IN MEMORIAM
MAUD

And Other Poems

ALFRED TENNYSON

———

NEW YORK

HURST & COMPANY

PUBLISHERS.

CONTENTS.

IN MEMORIAM.

———◆◆◆———

Strong Son of God, immortal Love,
   Whom we, that have not seen thy face,
   By faith, and faith alone, embrace,
Believing where we cannot prove;

Thine are these orbs of light and shade;
   Thou madest life in man and brute;
   Thou madest Death; and lo, thy foot
Is on the skull which thou hast made.

Thou wilt not leave us in the dust:
   Thou madest man, he knows not why,
   He thinks he was not made to die;
And thou hast made him: thou art just.

Thou seemest human and divine,
   The highest, holiest manhood, thou:
   Our wills are ours, we know not how;
Our wills are ours, to make them thine.

Our little systems have their day;
   They have their day and cease to be:
   They are but broken lights of thee,
And thou, O Lord, art more than they.

5

We have but faith; we cannot know;
　　For knowledge is of things we see;
　　And yet we trust it comes from thee,
A beam in darkness: let it grow.

Let knowledge grow from more to more,
　　But more of reverence in us dwell;
　　That mind and soul, according well,
May make one music as before,

But vaster.　We are fools and slight;
　　We mock thee when we do not fear:
　　But help thy foolish ones to bear;
Help thy vain worlds to bear thy light.

Forgive what seem'd my sin in me;
　　What seem'd my worth since I began;
　　For merit lives from man to man,
And not from man, O Lord, to thee.

Forgive my grief for one removed,
　　Thy creature, whom I found so fair.
　　I trust he lives in thee, and there
I find him worthier to be loved.

Forgive these wild and wandering cries,
　　Confusions of a wasted youth;
　　Forgive them where they fail in truth,
And in thy wisdom make me wise.

IN MEMORIAM.

A. H. H.

OBIIT MDCCCXXXIII.

I.

I HELD it truth, with him who sings
   To one clear harp in divers tones,
   That men may rise on stepping-stones
Of their dead selves to higher things.

But who shall so forecast the years,
   And find in loss a gain to match?
   Or reach a hand thro' time to catch
The far-off interest of tears?

Let Love clasp Grief lest both be drown'd,
   Let darkness keep her raven gloss:
   Ah, sweeter to be drunk with loss,
To dance with death, to beat the ground,

Than that the victor Hours should scorn
   The long result of love, and boast,
   "Behold the man that loved and lost
But all he was is overworn."

II.

OLD Yew, which graspest at the stones
　　That name the underlying dead,
　　Thy fibres net the dreamless head,
Thy roots are wrapt about the bones.

The seasons bring the flower again,
　　And bring the firstling to the flock;
　　And in the dusk of thee, the clock
Beats out the little lives of men.

O not for thee the glow, the bloom,
　　Who changest not in any gale,
　　Nor branding summer suns avail
To touch thy thousand years of gloom:

And gazing on thee, sullen tree,
　　Sick for thy stubborn hardihood,
　　I seem to fail from out my blood
And grow incorporate into thee.

III.

O SORROW, cruel fellowship,
　　O Priestess in the vaults of Death,
　　O sweet and bitter in a breath,
What whispers from thy lying lip?

"The stars," she whispers, "blindly run;
　　A web is wov'n across the sky:
　　From out waste places comes a cry,
And murmurs from the dying sun:

" And all the phantom, Nature, stands,
　　With all the music in her tone,
　　A hollow echo of my own, —
A hollow form with empty hands."

And shall I take a thing so blind,
　　Embrace her as my natural good;
　　Or crush her, like a vice of blood,
Upon the threshold of the mind?

IV.

To Sleep I give my powers away;
　　My will is bondsman to the dark;
　　I sit within a helmless bark,
And with my heart I muse and say:

O heart, how fares it with thee now,
　　That thou shouldst fail from thy desire,
　　Who scarcely darest to inquire
" What is it makes me beat so low?"

Something it is which thou hast lost,
　　Some pleasure from thine early years.
　　Break, thou deep vase of chilling tears,
That grief hath shaken into frost!

Such clouds of nameless trouble cross
　　All night below the darken'd eyes;
　　With morning wakes the will, and cries,
" Thou shalt not be the fool of loss."

V.

I SOMETIMES hold it half a sin
　To put in words the grief I feel;
　For words, like Nature, half reveal
And half conceal the Soul within.

But, for the unquiet heart and brain,
　A use in measured language lies;
　The sad mechanic exercise,
Like dull narcotics, numbing pain.

In words, like weeds, I'll wrap me o'er,
　Like coarsest clothes against the cold;
　But that large grief which these enfold
Is given in outline and no more.

VI.

ONE writes, that "Other friends remain,"
　That "Loss is common to the race," —
　And common is the commonplace,
And vacant chaff well meant for grain.

That loss is common would not make
　My own less bitter, rather more:
　Too common! Never morning wore
To evening, but some heart did break.

O father, whereso'er thou be,
　Who pledgest now thy gallant son;
　A shot, ere half thy draught be done,
Hath still'd the life that beat from thee.

O mother, praying God will save
   Thy sailor, — while thy head is bow'd,
   His heavy-shotted hammock-shroud
Drops in his vast and wandering grave.

Ye know no more than I who wrought
   At that last hour to please him well;
   Who mused on all I had to tell,
And something written, something thought.

Expecting still his advent home:
   And ever met him on his way
   With wishes, thinking, here to-day,
Or here to-morrow will he come.

O somewhere, meek unconscious dove,
   That sittest ranging golden hair;
   And glad to find thyself so fair,
Poor child, that waitest for thy love!

For now her father's chimney glows
   In expectation of a guest
   And thinking "This will please him best,"
She takes a ribbon or a rose;

For he will see them on to-night;
   And with the thought her color burns;
   And, having left the glass, she turns
Once more to set a ringlet right;

And, even when she turn'd, the curse
   Had fallen, and her future lord
   Was drown'd in passing thro' the ford,
Or kill'd in falling from his horse.

O what to her shall be the end?
   And what to me remains of good?
   To her, perpetual maidenhood,
And unto me no second friend.

VII.

DARK house, by which once more I stand
   Here in the long unlovely street,
   Doors, where my heart was used to beat
So quickly, waiting for a hand,

A hand that can be clasp'd no more, —
   Behold me, for I cannot sleep,
   And like a guilty thing I creep
At earliest morning to the door.

He is not here; but far away
   The noise of life begins again,
   And ghastly thro' the drizzling rain
On the bald street breaks the blank day.

VIII.

A HAPPY lover who has come
   To look on her that loves him well,
   Who 'lights and rings the gateway bell,
And learns her gone and far from home;

He saddens, all the magic light
  Dies off at once from bower and hall,
  And all the place is dark, and all
The chambers emptied of delight;

So find I every pleasant spot
  In which we two were wont to meet,
  The field, the chamber, and the street,
For all is dark where thou art not.

Yet as that other, wandering there
  In those deserted walks, may find
  A flower beat with rain and wind,
Which once she foster'd up with care;

So seems it in my deep regret,
  O my forsaken heart, with thee
  And this poor flower of poesy
Which little cared for fades not yet.

But since it pleased a vanish'd eye,
  I go to plant it on his tomb,
  That if it can it there may bloom,
Or dying, there at least may die.

IX.

FAIR ship, that from the Italian shore
  Sailest the placid ocean-plains
  With my lost Arthur's loved remains,
Spread thy full wings, and waft him o'er.

So draw him home to those that mourn
   In vain; a favorable speed
   Ruffle thy mirror'd mast, and lead
Thro' prosperous floods his holy urn.

All night no ruder air perplex
   Thy sliding keel, till Phosphor, bright
   As our pure love, thro' early light
Shall glimmer on the dewy decks.

Sphere all your lights around, above;
   Sleep, gentle heavens, before the prow;
   Sleep, gentle winds, as he sleeps now,
My friend, the brother of my love;

My Arthur, whom I shall not see
   Till all my widow'd race be run;
   Dear as the mother to the son,
More than my brothers are to me.

X.

I HEAR the noise about thy keel;
   I hear the bell struck in the night;
   I see the cabin-window bright;
I see the sailor at the wheel.

Thou bringest the sailor to his wife,
   And travell'd men from foreign lands;
   And letters unto trembling hands;
And, thy dark freight, a vanish'd life.

So bring him: we have idle dreams:
  This look of quiet flatters thus
  Our home-bred fancies: O to us,
The fools of habit, sweeter seems

To rest beneath the clover sod,
  That takes the sunshine and the rains,
  Or where the kneeling hamlet drains
The chalice of the grapes of God;

Then if with thee the roaring wells
  Should gulf him fathom deep in brine;
  And hands so often clasp'd in mine
Should toss with tangle and with shells.

XI.

CALM is the morn without a sound,
  Calm as to suit a calmer grief,
  And only thro' the faded leaf
The chestnut pattering to the ground:

Calm and deep peace on this high wold
  And on these dews that drench the furze,
  And all the silvery gossamers
That twinkle into green and gold:

Calm and still light on yon great plain
  That sweeps with all its autumn bowers,
  And crowded farms and lessening towers,
To mingle with the bounding main;

Calm and deep peace in this wide air,
　　These leaves that redden to the fall;
　　And in my heart, if calm at all,
If any calm, a calm despair:

Calm on the seas, and silver sleep,
　　And waves that sway themselves in rest,
　　And dead calm in that noble breast
Which heaves but with the heaving deep.

XII.

Lo, as a dove when up she springs
　　To bear thro' Heaven a tale of woe,
　　Some dolorous message knit below
The wild pulsation of her wings;

Like her I go; I cannot stay;
　　I leave this mortal ark behind,
　　A weight of nerves without a mind,
And leave the cliffs, and haste away

O'er ocean-mirrors rounded large,
　　And reach the glow of southern skies,
　　And see the sails at a distance rise,
And linger weeping on the marge,

And saying, "Comes he thus, my friend?
　　Is this the end of all my care?"
　　And circle moaning in the air:
"Is this the end? Is this the end?"

And forward dart again, and play
   About the prow, and back return
   To where the body sits, and learn,
That I have been an hour away.

XIII.

TEARS of the widower, when he sees
   A late-lost form that sleep reveals,
   And moves his doubtful arms, and feels
Her place is empty, fall like these;

Which weep a loss forever new,
   A void where heart on heart reposed;
   And, where warm hands have prest and clos'd,
Silence, till I be silent too.

Which weep the comrade of my choice
   An awful thought, a life removed,
   The human-hearted man I loved,
A Spirit, not a breathing voice.

Come Time, and teach me, many years,
   I do not suffer in a dream;
   For now so strange do these things seem
Mine eyes have leisure for their tears;

My fancies time to rise on wing,
   And glance about the approaching sails,
   As tho' they brought but merchants' bales,
And not the burthen that they bring.

XIV.

If one should bring me this report,
    That thou hadst touch'd the land to-day,
    And I went down unto the quay,
And found thee lying in the port;

And standing, muffled round with woe,
    Should see thy passengers in rank
    Come stepping lightly down the plank,
And beckoning unto those they know;

And if along with these should come
    The man I held as half divine;
    Should strike a sudden hand in mine,
And ask a thousand things of home;

And I should tell him all my pain,
    And how my life had droop'd of late,
    And he should sorrow o'er my state
And marvel what possess'd my brain;

And I perceived no touch of change,
    No hint of death in all his frame,
    But found him all in all the same,
I should not feel it to be strange.

XV.

To-night the winds begin to rise
    And roar from yonder dropping day;
    The last red leaf is whirl'd away,
The rooks are blown about the skies;

The forest crack'd, the waters curl'd,
  The cattle huddled on the lea;
  And wildly dash'd on tower and tree
The sunbeam strikes along the world:

And but for fancies, which aver
  That all thy motions gently pass
  Athwart a plane of molten glass,
I scarce could brook the strain and stir

That makes the barren branches loud;
  And but for fear it is not so,
  The wild unrest that lives in woe
Would dote and pore on yonder cloud

That rises upward always higher,
  And onward drags a laboring breast,
  And topples round the dreary west,
A looming bastion fringed with fire.

XVI.

WHAT words are these have fall'n from me?
  Can calm despair and wild unrest
  Be tenants of a single breast,
Or sorrow such a changeling be?

Or doth she only seem to take
  The touch of change in calm or storm;
  But knows no more of transient form
In her deep self, than some dead lake

That holds the shadow of a lark
  Hung in the shadow of a heaven?
  Or has the shock, so harshly given,
Confused me like the unhappy bark

That strikes by night a craggy shelf,
  And staggers blindly ere she sink?
  And stunn'd me from my power to think
And all my knowledge of myself;

And made me that delirious man
  Whose fancy fuses old and new,
  And flashes into false and true,
And mingles all without a plan?

XVII.

THOU comest, much wept for: such a breeze
  Compell'd thy canvas, and my prayer
  Was as the whisper of an air
To breathe thee over lonely seas.

For I in spirit saw thee move
  Thro' circles of the bounding sky,
  Week after week: the days go by:
Come quick, thou bringest all I love.

Henceforth, wherever thou may'st roam,
  My blessing, like a line of light,
  Is on the waters day and night,
And like a beacon guards thee home.

So may whatever tempest mars
  Mid-ocean spare thee, sacred bark;
  And balmy drops in summer dark
Slide from the bosom of the stars.

So kind an office hath been done,
  Such precious relics brought by thee;
  The dust of him I shall not see
Till all my widow'd race be run.

XVIII.

'Tis well; 'tis something; we may stand
  Where he in English earth is laid,
  And from his ashes may be made
The violet of his native land.

'Tis little; but it looks in truth
  As if the quiet bones were blest
  Among familiar names to rest
And in the places of his youth.

Come then, pure hands, and bear the head
  That sleeps or wears the mask of sleep,
  And come, whatever loves to weep,
And hear the ritual of the dead.

Ah yet, ev'n yet, if this might be,
  I, falling on his faithful heart,
  Would breathing through his lips impart
The life that almost dies in me;

That dies not, but endures with pain,
  And slowly forms the firmer mind,
  Treasuring the look it cannot find,
The words that are not heard again.

XIX.

THE Danube to the Severn gave
  The darken'd heart that beat no more;
  They laid him by the pleasant shore,
And in the hearing of the wave.

There twice a day the Severn fills;
  The salt sea-water passes by,
  And hushes half the babbling Wye,
And makes a silence in the hills.

The Wye is hush'd nor moved along,
  And hush'd by deepest grief of all,
  When fill'd with tears that cannot fall,
I brim with sorrow drowning song.

The tide flows down, the wave again
  Is vocal in its wooded walls;
  My deeper anguish also falls
And I can speak a little then.

XX.

THE lesser griefs that may be said,
  That breathe a thousand tender vows,
  Are but as servants in a house
Where lies the master newly dead;

Who speak their feeling as it is,
  And weep the fulness from the mind:
  "It will be hard," they say, "to find
Another service such as this."

My lighter moods are like to these,
  That out of words a comfort win;
  But there are other griefs within,
And tears that at their fountain freeze:

For by the hearth the children sit
  Cold in that atmosphere of Death,
  And scarce endure to draw the breath,
Or like to noiseless phantoms flit:

But open converse is there none,
  So much the vital spirits sink
  To see the vacant chair, and think,
"How good! how kind! and he is gone."

XXI.

I SING to him that rests below,
  And, since the grasses round me wave,
  I take the grasses of the grave,
And make them pipes whereon to blow.

The traveller hears me now and then,
  And sometimes harshly will he speak:
  "This fellow would make weakness weak,
And melt the waxen hearts of men."

Another answers, " Let him be,
   He loves to make parade of pain,
   That with his piping he may gain
The praise that comes to constancy."

A third is wroth, " Is this an hour
   For private sorrow's barren song,
   When more and more the people throng
The chairs and thrones of civil power?

" A time to sicken and to swoon,
   When Science reaches forth her arms
   To feel from world to world, and charms
Her secret from the latest moon?"

Behold, ye speak an idle thing:
   Ye never knew the sacred dust;
   I do but sing because I must,
And pipe but as the linnets sing:

And one is glad; her note is gay,
   For now her little ones have ranged;
   And one is sad; her note is changed,
Because her brood is stol'n away.

XXII.

THE path by which we twain did go,
   Which led by tracts that pleased us well,
   Thro' four sweet years arose and fell,
From flower to flower, from snow to snow:

And we with singing cheer'd the way,
   And crown'd with all the season lent,
   From April on to April went,
And glad at heart from May to May:

But where the path we walk'd began
   To slant the fifth autumnal slope,
   As we descended, following Hope,
There sat the Shadow fear'd of man;

Who broke our fair companionship,
   And spread his mantle dark and cold,
   And wrapt thee formless in the fold,
And dull'd the murmur on thy lip,

And bore thee where I could not see
   Nor follow, tho' I walk in haste,
   And think that somewhere in the waste
The Shadow sits and waits for me.

XXIII.

Now, sometimes in my sorrow shut,
   Or breaking into song by fits,
   Alone, alone, to where he sits,
The Shadow cloak'd from head to foot,

Who keeps the keys of all the creeds,
   I wander, often falling lame,
   And looking back to whence I came,
Or on to where the pathway leads;

And crying, "How changed from where it ran
　　Thro' lands where not a leaf was dumb;
　　But all the lavish hills would hum
The murmur of a happy Pan:

"When each by turns was guide to each,
　　And Fancy light from Fancy caught,
　　And Thought leapt out to wed with Thought
Ere Thought could wed itself with Speech;

"And all we met was fair and good,
　　And all was good that Time could bring,
　　And all the secret of the Spring
Moved in the chambers of the blood;

"And many an old philosophy
　　On Argive heights divinely sang,
　　And round us all the thicket rang
To many a flute of Arcady."

XXIV.

AND was the day of my delight
　　As sure and perfect as I say?
　　The very source and fount of Day
Is dash'd with wandering isles of night.

If all was good and fair we met,
　　This earth had been the Paradise
　　It never look'd to human eyes
Since Adam left his garden yet.

And is it that the haze of grief
   Makes former gladness loom so great?
   The lowness of the present state,
That sets the past in this relief?

Or that the past will always win
   A glory from its being far;
   An orb into the perfect star
We saw not, when we moved therein?

XXV.

I KNOW that this was Life, — the track
   Whereon with equal feet we fared;
   And then, as now, the day prepared
The daily burden for the back.

But this it was that made me move
   As light as carrier-birds in air;
   I loved the weight I had to bear,
Because I needed help of love;

Nor could I weary, heart or limb,
   When mighty Love would cleave in twain
   The lading of a single pain,
And part it, giving half to him.

XXVI.

STILL onward winds the weary way;
   I with it; for I long to prove
   No lapse of moons can canker Love,
Whatever fickle tongues may say.

And if that eye which watches guilt
   And goodness, and hath power to see
   Within the green the moulder'd tree
And towers fall'n as soon as built, —

O, if indeed that eye foresee
   ·Or see (in Him is no before)
   In more of life true life no more,
And Love the indifference to be,

Then might I find, ere yet the morn
   Breaks hither over Indian seas,
   That shadow waiting with the keys,
To shroud me from my proper scorn.

XXVII.

I ENVY not in any moods
   The captive void of noble rage,
   The linnet born within the cage,
That never knew the summer woods:

I envy not the beast that takes
   His license in the field of time,
   Unfetter'd by the sense of crime,
To whom a conscience never wakes:

Nor, what may count itself as blest,
   The heart that never plighted troth,
   But stagnates in the weeds of sloth
Nor any want-begotten rest.

I hold it true, whate'er befall;
  I feel it, when I sorrow most;
  'Tis better to have loved and lost
Than never to have loved at all.

XXVIII.

THE time draws near the birth of Christ;
  The moon is hid; the night is still;
  The Christmas bells from hill to hill
Answer each other in the mist.

Four voices of four hamlets round,
  From far and near, on mead and moor,
  Swell out and fail, as if a door
Were shut between me and the sound:

Each voice four changes on the wind,
  That now dilate, and now decrease,
  Peace and good-will, good-will and peace,
Peace and good-will, to all mankind.

This year I slept and woke with pain,
  I almost wish'd no more to wake,
  And that my hold on life would break
Before I heard those bells again:

But they my troubled spirit rule,
  For they controll'd me when a boy;
  They bring me sorrow touch'd with joy,
The merry, merry bells of Yule.

XXIX.

WITH such compelling cause to grieve
  As daily vexes household peace,
  And chains regret to his decease,
How dare we keep our Christmas-eve

Which brings no more a welcome guest
  To enrich the threshold of the night
  With shower'd largess of delight,
In dance and song and game and jest.

Yet go, and while the holly-boughs
  Entwine the cold baptismal font,
  Make one wreath more for Use and Wont
That guard the portals of the house;

Old sister of a day gone by,
  Gray nurses, loving nothing new;
  Why should they miss their yearly due
Before their time? They too will die.

XXX.

WITH trembling fingers did we weave
  The holly round the Christmas hearth;
  A rainy cloud possess'd the earth,
And sadly fell on Christmas-eve.

At our old pastimes in the hall
  We gamboll'd, making vain pretence
  Of gladness, with an awful sense
Of one mute Shadow watching all.

We paused: the winds were in the beech;
  We heard them sweep the winter land;
  And in a circle hand-in-hand
Sat silent, looking each at each.

Then echo-like our voices rang;
  We sung tho' every eye was dim,
  A merry song we sang with him
Last year: impetuously we sang:

We ceased: a gentler feeling crept
  Upon us: surely rest is meet:
  "They rest," we said, "their sleep is sweet,"
And silence follow'd, and we wept.

Our voices took a higher range;
  Once more we sang: "They do not die
  Nor lose their mortal sympathy,
Nor change to us, although they change;

"Rapt from the fickle and the frail
  With gather'd power, yet the same,
  Pierces the keen seraphic flame
From orb to orb, from veil to veil."

Rise, happy morn, rise, holy morn,
  Draw forth the cheerful day from night:
  O father, touch the east, and light
The light that shone when Hope was born.

XXXI.

WHEN Lazarus left his charnel-cave,
　　And home to Mary's house return'd,
　　Was this demanded,— if he yearn'd
To hear her weeping by his grave?

"Where wert thou, brother, those four **days?**"
　　There lives no record of reply,
　　Which telling what it is to die
Had surely added praise to praise.

From every house the neighbors met,
　　The streets were fill'd with joyful **sound,**
　　A solemn gladness even crown'd
The purple brows of Olivet.

Behold a man raised up by Christ!
　　The rest remaineth unreveal'd;
　　He told it not; or something seal'd
The lips of that Evangelist.

XXXII.

HER eyes are homes of silent prayer,
　　Nor other thought her mind admits
　　But, he was dead, and there he sits,
And he that brought him back is there.

Then one deep love doth supersede
　　All other, when her ardent gaze
　　Roves from the living brother's face,
And rests upon the Life indeed.

All subtle thought, all curious fears,
  Borne down by gladness so complete,
  She bows, she bathes the Saviour's feet
With costly spikenard and with tears.

Thrice blest whose lives are faithful prayers,
  Whose loves in higher love endure;
  What souls possess themselves so pure,
Or is there blessedness like theirs?

XXXIII.

O THOU that after toil and storm
  Mayst seem to have reach'd a purer air,
  Whose faith has centre everywhere,
Nor cares to fix itself to form,

Leave thou thy sister, when she prays,
  Her early Heaven, her happy views;
  Nor thou with shadow'd hint confuse
A life that leads melodious days.

Her faith thro' form is pure as thine,
  Her hands are quicker unto good:
  O, sacred be the flesh and blood
To which she links a truth divine!

See thou, that contest reason ripe
  In holding by the law within,
  Thou fail not in a world of sin,
And ev'n for want of such a type.

XXXIV.

My own dim life should teach me this,
   That life shall live forevermore,
   Else earth is darkness at the core,
And dust and ashes all that is:

This round of green, this orb of flame,
   Fantastic beauty; such as lurks
   In some wild Poet, when he works
Without a conscience or an aim.

What then were God to such as I?
   'Twere hardly worth my while to choose
   Of things all mortal, or to use
A little patience ere I die;

'Twere best at once to sink to peace,
   Like birds the charming serpent draws,
   To drop head foremost in the jaws
Of vacant darkness, and to cease.

XXXV.

Yet if some voice that man could trust
   Should murmur from the narrow house,
   "The cheeks drop in; the body bows;
Man dies: nor is there hope in dust:"

Might I not say, "Yet even here,
   But for one hour, O Love, I strive
   To keep so sweet a thing alive?"
But I should turn mine ears and hear

The moanings of the homeless sea,
  The sound of streams that swift or slow
  Draw down Æonian hills, and sow
The dust of continents to be;

And Love would answer with a sigh,
  "The sound of that forgetful shore
  Will change my sweetness more and more,
Half-dead to know that I shall die."

O me! what profits it to put
  An idle case? If Death were seen
  At first as Death, Love had not been,
Or been in narrowest working shut,

Mere fellowship of sluggish moods,
  Or in his coarsest Satyr-shape
  Had bruised the herb and crush'd the grape,
And bask'd and batten'd in the woods.

XXXVI.

THO' truths in manhood darkly join,
  Deep-seated in our mystic frame,
  We yield all blessing to the name
Of Him that made them current coin;

For Wisdom dealt with mortal powers,
  Where truth in closest words shall fail,
  When truth embodied in a tale
Shall enter in at lowly doors.

And so the Word had breath, and wrought
  With human hands the creed of creeds
  In loveliness of perfect deeds,
More strong than all poetic thought;

Which he may read that binds the sheaf,
  Or builds the house, or digs the grave,
  And those wild eyes that watch the wave
In roarings round the coral reef.

XXXVII.

URANIA speaks with darken'd brow;
  "Thou pratest here where thou art least;
  This faith has many a purer priest,
And many an abler voice than thou.

"Go down beside thy native rill,
  On thy Parnassus set thy feet,
  And hear thy laurel whisper sweet
About the ledges of the hill."

And my Melpomene replies,
  A touch of shame upon her cheek:
  "I am not worthy ev'n to speak
Of thy prevailing mysteries;

"For I am but an earthly Muse,
  And owning but a little art
  To lull with song an aching heart,
And render human love his dues;

" But brooding on the dear one dead,
    And all he said of things divine,
    (And dear to me as sacred wine
To dying lips is all he said,)

" I murmur'd, as I came along,
    Of comfort clasp'd in truth reveal'd;
    And loiter'd in the Master's field,
And darken'd sanctities with song."

XXXVIII.

WITH weary steps I loiter on,
    Tho' always under alter'd skies
    The purple from the distance dies,
My prospect and horizon gone.

No joy the blowing season gives,
    The herald melodies of spring,
    But in the songs I love to sing
A doubtful gleam of solace lives.

If any care for what is here
    Survive in spirits render'd free,
    Then are these songs I sing of thee
Not all ungrateful to thine ear.

XXXIX.

COULD we forget the widow'd hour,
    And look on Spirits breathed away,
    As on a maiden in the day
When first she wears her orange-flower!

When crown'd with blessing she doth rise
    To take her latest leave of home,
    And hopes and light regrets that come
Make April of her tender eyes;

And doubtful joys the father move,
    And tears are on the mother's face,
    As parting with a long embrace
She enters other realms of love:

Her office there to rear, to teach,
    Becoming, as is meet and fit,
    A link among the days, to knit
The generations each with each;

And, doubtless, unto thee is given
    A life that bears immortal fruit
    In such great offices as suit
The full-grown energies of heaven.

Ay me, the difference I discern!
    How often shall her old fireside
    Be cheer'd with tidings of the bride,
How often she herself return,

And tell them all they would have told,
    And bring her babe, and make her boast
    Till even those that miss'd her most
Shall count new things as dear as old:

But thou and I have shaken hands,
  Till growing winters lay me low;
  My paths are in the fields I know,
And thine in undiscover'd lands.

XL.

THY spirit ere our fatal loss
  Did ever rise from high to higher:
  As mounts the heavenward altar-fire,
As flies the lighter thro' the gross.

But thou art turn'd to something strange.
  And I have lost the links that bound
  Thy changes; here upon the ground,
No more partaker of thy change.

Deep folly! yet that this could be,—
  That I could wing my will with might
  To leap the grades of life and light,
And flash at once, my friend, to thee;

For tho' my nature rarely yields
  To that vague fear implied in death;
  Nor shudders at the gulfs beneath,
The howlings from forgotten fields:

Yet oft when sundown skirts the moor
  An inner trouble I behold,
  A spectral doubt which makes me cold,
That I shall be thy mate no more,

Tho' following with an upward mind
  The wonders that have come to thee,
  Thro' all the secular to-be,
But evermore a life behind.

XLI.

I VEX my heart with fancies dim:
  He still outstript me in the race;
  It was but unity of place
That made me dream I rank'd with him.

And so may Place retain us still,
  And he the much-beloved again,
  A lord of large experience, train
To riper growth the mind and will:

And what delights can equal those
  That stir the spirit's inner deeps,
  When one that loves, but knows not, reaps
A truth from one that loves and knows?

XLII.

IF Sleep and Death be truly one,
  And every spirit's folded bloom
  Thro' all its intervital gloom
In some long trance should slumber on;

Unconscious of the sliding hour,
  Bare of the body, might it last,
  And silent traces of the past
Be all the color of the flower:

So then were nothing lost to **man**;
 So that still garden of the souls
 In many a figured leaf enrolls
The total world since life began;

And love will last as pure and whole
 As when he loved me here in **Time**,
 And at the spiritual prime
Rewaken with the dawning soul.

XLIII

How fares it with the happy dead?
 For here the man is more and **more**;
 But he forgets the days before
God shut the doorways of his head.

The days have vanish'd, tone and tint,
 And yet perhaps the hoarding sense
 Gives out at times (he knows not **whence)**
A little flash, a mystic hint;

And in the long harmonious years
 (If Death so taste Lethean springs)
 May some dim touch of earthly things
Surprise thee ranging with thy peers.

If such a dreamy touch should fall,
 O turn thee round, resolve the doubt;
 My guardian angel will speak out
In that high place, and tell thee all.

XLIV.

THE baby new to earth and sky,
  What time his tender palm is prest
  Against the circle of the breast,
Has never thought that "this is I:"

But as he grows he gathers much,
  And learns the use of "I," and "me,"
  And finds "I am not what I see,
And other than the things I touch."

So rounds he to a separate mind
  From whence clear memory may begin,
  As thro' the frame that binds him in
His isolation grows defined.

This use may lie in blood and breath,
  Which else were fruitless of their due,
  Had man to learn himself anew,
Beyond the second birth of Death.

XLV.

WE ranging down the lower track,
  The path we came by, thorn and flower,
  Is shadow'd by the growing hour,
Lest life should fail in looking back.

So be it: there no shade can last
  In that deep dawn behind the tomb,
  But clear from marge to marge shall bloom
The eternal landscape of the past:

A lifelong tract of time reveal'd;
   The fruitful hours of still increase;
   Days order'd in a wealthy peace,
And those five years its richest field.

Oh Love, thy province were not large,
   A bounded field, nor stretching far;
   Look also, Love, a brooding star,
A rosy warmth from marge to marge.

XLVI.

THAT each, who seems a separate whole,
   Should move his rounds, and fusing all
   The skirts of self again, should fall
Remerging in the general Soul,

Is faith as vague as all unsweet:
   Eternal form shall still divide
   The eternal soul from all beside;
And I shall know him when we meet:

And we shall sit at endless feast,
   Enjoying each the other's good:
   What vaster dream can hit the mood
Of Love on earth? He seeks at least

Upon the last and sharpest height,
   Before the spirits fade away,
   Some landing-place, to clasp and say,
"Farewell! We lose ourselves in light."

XLVII.

IF these brief lays, of Sorrow born,
    Were taken to be such as closed
    Grave doubts and answers here proposed,
Then these were such as men might scorn:

Her care is not to part and prove;
    She takes, when harsher moods remit,
    What slender shade of doubt may flit,
And makes it vassal unto love:

And hence, indeed, she sports with words,
    But better serves a wholesome law,
    And holds it sin and shame to draw
The deepest measure from the chords:

Nor dare she trust a larger lay,
    But rather loosens from the lip
    Short swallow-flights of song, that dip
Their wings in tears, and skim away.

XLVIII.

FROM art, from nature, from the schools,
    Let random influences glance,
    Like light in many a shiver'd lance
That breaks about the dappled pools:

The lightest wave of thought shall lisp,
    The fancy's tenderest eddy wreathe,
    The slightest air of song shall breathe
To make the sullen surface crisp.

And look thy look, and go thy way,
　But blame not thou the winds that make
　The seeming-wanton ripple break,
The tender-pencil'd shadow play.

Beneath all fancied hopes and fears,
　Ay me! the sorrow deepens down,
　Whose muffled motions blindly drown
The bases of my life in tears.

XLIX.

BE near me when my light is low,
　When the blood creeps, and the nerves prick
　And tingle; and the heart is sick,
And all the wheels of Being slow.

Be near me when the sensuous frame
　Is rack'd with pangs that conquer trust:
　And Time, a maniac scattering dust,
And Life, a Fury slinging flame.

Be near me when my faith is dry,
　And men the flies of latter spring,
　That lay their eggs, and sting and sing,
And weave their petty cells and die.

Be near me when I fade away,
　To point the term of human strife,
　And on the low dark verge of life
The twilight of eternal day.

L.

Do we indeed desire the dead
   Should still be near us at our side?
   Is there no baseness we would hide?
No inner vileness that we dread?

Should he for whose applause I strove,
   I had such reverence for his blame,
   See with clear eye some hidden shame,
And I be lessen'd in his love?

I wrong the grave with fears untrue:
   Shall love be blamed for want of faith?
   There must be wisdom with great Death
The dead shall look me thro' and thro'.

Be near us when we climb or fall:
   Ye watch, like God, the rolling hours
   With larger other eyes than ours,
To make allowance for us all.

LI.

I CANNOT love thee as I ought,
   For love reflects the thing beloved;
   My words are only words, and moved
Upon the topmost froth of thought.

" Yet blame not thou thy plaintive song,"
   The Spirit of true love replied;
   " Thou canst not move me from thy side,
Nor human frailty do me wrong.

" What keeps a spirit wholly true
   To that ideal which he bears?
   What record? not the sinless years
That breathed beneath the Syrian blue:

" So fret not, like an idle girl,
   That life is dash'd with flecks of sin.
   Abide: thy wreath is gather'd in,
When Time hath sunder'd shell from pearl."

LII.

How many a father have I seen,
   A sober man among his boys,
   Whose youth was full of foolish noise,
Who wears his manhood hale and green:

And dare we to this fancy give,
   That had the wild-oat not been sown,
   The soil, left barren, scarce had grown
The grain by which a man may live?

O, if we held the doctrine sound
   For life outliving heats of youth,
   Yet who would preach it as a truth
To those that eddy round and round?

Hold thou the good: define it well;
   For fear divine Philosophy
   Should push beyond her mark, and be
Procuress to the Lords of Hell.

LIII.

O YET we trust that somehow good
  Will be the final goal of ill,
  To pangs of nature, sins of will,
Defects of doubt, and taints of blood;

That nothing walks with aimless feet;
  That not one life shall be destroy'd,
  Or cast as rubbish to the void,
When God hath made the pile complete;

That not a worm is cloven in vain;
  That not a moth with vain desire
  Is shrivell'd in a fruitless fire,
Or but subserves another's gain.

Behold we know not anything;
  I can but trust that good shall fall
  At last — far off — at last, to all,
And every winter change to spring.

So runs my dream: but what am I?
  An infant crying in the night:
  An infant crying for the light:
And with no language but a cry.

LIV.

THE wish, that of the living whole
  No life may fail beyond the grave,
  Derives it not from what we have
The likest God within the soul?

Are God and Nature then at strife,
　That Nature lends such evil dreams?
　So careful of the type she seems,
So careless of the single life;

That I, considering everywhere
　Her secret meaning in her deeds,
　And finding that of fifty seeds
She often brings but one to bear,

I falter where I firmly trod,
　And falling with my weight of cares
　Upon the great world's altar-stairs
That slope thro' darkness up to God,

I stretch lame hands of faith, and grope,
　And gather dust and chaff, and call
　To what I feel is Lord of all,
And faintly trust the larger hope.

LV.

"So careful of the type?" but no.
　From scarped cliff and quarried stone
　She cries, "A thousand types are gone:
I care for nothing, all shall go.

"Thou makest thine appeal to me:
　I bring to life, I bring to death:
　The spirit does but mean the breath:
I know no more." And he, shall he,

Man, her last work, who seem'd so fair,
  Such splendid purpose in his eyes,
  Who roll'd the psalm to wintry skies,
Who built him fanes of fruitless prayer,

Who trusted God was love indeed,
  And love Creation's final law, —
  Tho' Nature, red in tooth and claw
With ravin, shriek'd against his creed, —

Who loved, who suffer'd countless ills,
  Who battled for the True, the Just,
  Be blown about the desert dust,
Or seal'd within the iron hills?

No more? A monster then, a dream,
  A discord. Dragons of the prime,
  That tear each other in their slime,
Were mellow music match'd with him.

O life as futile, then, as frail!
  O for thy voice to soothe and bless!
  What hope of answer, or redress?
Behind the veil, behind the veil.

LVI.

PEACE; come away: the song of woe
  Is after all an earthly song:
  Peace; come away: we do him wrong
To sing so wildly: let us go.

Come; let us go: your cheeks are pale;
　But half my life I leave behind:
　Methinks my friend is richly shrined:
But I shall pass; my work will fail.

Yet in these ears, till hearing dies,
　One set slow bell will seem to toll
　The passing of the sweetest soul
That ever look'd with human eyes.

I hear it now, and o'er and o'er,
　Eternal greetings to the dead;
　And " Ave, Ave, Ave," said,
" Adieu, adieu," forevermore.

LVII.

IN those sad words I took farewell:
　Like echoes in sepulchral halls,
　As drop by drop the water falls
In vaults and catacombs they fell;

And, falling, idly broke the peace
　Of hearts that beat from day to day,
　Half conscious of their dying clay,
And those cold crypts where they shall **cease.**

The high Muse answer'd: " Wherefore grieve
　Thy brethren with a fruitless tear?
　Abide a little longer here,
And thou shalt take a nobler leave."

LVIII.

O SORROW, wilt thou live with me,
  No casual mistress, but a wife,
  My bosom-friend and half of life,
As I confess it needs must be;

O Sorrow, wilt thou rule my blood,
  Be sometimes lovely like a bride,
  And put thy harsher moods aside,
If thou wilt have me wise and good.

My centred passion cannot move,
  Nor will it lessen from to-day;
  But I'll have leave at times to play
As with the creature of my love:

And set thee forth, for thou art mine,
  With so much hope for years to come,
  That, howsoe'er I know thee, some
Could hardly tell what name were thine.

LIX.

HE past: a soul of nobler tone:
  My spirit loved and loves him yet,
  Like some poor girl whose heart is set
On one whose rank exceeds her own.

He mixing with his proper sphere,
  She finds the baseness of her lot,
  Half jealous of she knows not what,
And envying all that meet him there.

The little village looks forlorn;
  She sighs amid her narrow days,
  Moving about the household ways,
In that dark house where she was born

The foolish neighbors come and go,
  And tease her till the day draws by:
  At night she weeps, "How vain am I!
How should he love a thing so low?"

LX.

IF, in thy second state sublime,
  Thy ransom'd reason change replies
  With all the circle of the wise,
The perfect flower of human time:

And if thou cast thine eyes below,
  How dimly character'd and slight,
  How dwarf'd a growth of cold and night,
How blanch'd with darkness must I grow!

Yet turn thee to the doubtful shore,
  Where thy first form was made a man;
  I loved thee, Spirit, and love, nor can
The soul of Shakespeare love thee more.

LXI.

THO' if an eye that's downward cast
  Could make thee somewhat blench or fail,
  Then be my love an idle tale,
And fading legend of the past;

And thou as one that once declined
   When he was little more than boy,
   On some unworthy heart with joy,
But lives to wed an equal mind;

And breathes a novel world, the while
   His other passion wholly dies,
   Or in the light of deeper eyes
Is matter for a flying smile.

LXII.

YET pity for a horse o'er-driven,
   And love in which my hound has part,
   Can hang no weight upon my heart
In its assumptions up to heaven;

And I am so much more than these,
   As thou, perchance, art more than I,
   And yet I spare them sympathy,
And I would set their pains at ease.

So mayst thou watch me where I weep
   As unto vaster motions bound,
   The circuits of thine orbit round
A higher height, a deeper deep.

LXIII.

DOST thou look back on what hath been,
   As some divinely gifted man,
   Whose life in low estate began
And on a simple village green;

Who breaks his birth's invidious bar,
   And grasps the skirts of happy chance,
   And breasts the blows of circumstance,
And grapples with his evil star;

Who makes by force his merit known,
   And lives to clutch the golden keys
   To mould a mighty state's decrees,
And shape the whisper of the throne;

And moving up from high to higher,
   Becomes on Fortune's crowning slope
   The pillar of a people's hope,
The centre of a world's desire;

Yet feels, as in a pensive dream,
   When all his active powers are still,
   A distant dearness in the hill,
A secret sweetness in the stream,

The limit of his narrower fate,
   While yet beside its vocal springs
   He play'd at counsellors and kings,
With one that was his earliest mate;

Who ploughs with pain his native lea
   And reaps the labor of his hands,
   Or in the furrow musing stands:
"Does my old friend remember me?"

LXIV.

Sweet soul, do with me as thou wilt;
  I lull a fancy trouble-tost
  With "Love's too precious to be lost,
A little grain shall not be spilt."

And in that solace can I sing,
  Till out of painful phases wrought
  There flutters up a happy thought,
Self-balanced on a lightsome wing:

Since we deserved the name of friends,
  And thine effect so lives in me,
  A part of mine may live in thee,
And move thee on to noble ends.

LXV.

You thought my heart too far diseased;
  You wonder when my fancies play
  To find me gay among the gay,
Like one with any trifle pleased.

The shade by which my life was crost,
  Which makes a desert in the mind,
  Has made me kindly with my kind,
And like to him whose sight is lost;

Whose feet are guided thro' the land,
  Whose jest among his friends is free,
  Who takes the children on his knee,
And winds their curls about his hand:

He plays with threads, he beats his chair
For pastime, dreaming of the sky;
His inner day can never die,
His night of loss is always there.

LXVI.

WHEN on my bed the moonlight falls,
I know that in thy place of rest,
By that broad water of the west,
There comes a glory on the walls:

Thy marble bright in dark appears,
As slowly steals a silver flame
Along the letters of thy name,
And o'er the number of thy years.

The mystic glory swims away:
From off my bed the moonlight dies;
And, closing eaves of wearied eyes,
I sleep till dusk is dipt in gray:

And then I know the mist is drawn
A lucid veil from coast to coast,
And in the dark church, like a ghost,
Thy tablet glimmers to the dawn.

LXVII.

WHEN in the down I sink my head,
Sleep, Death's twin-brother, times my breath;
Sleep, Death's twin-brother, knows not Death,
Nor can I dream of thee as dead:

I walk as ere I walk'd forlorn,
　　When all our path was fresh with dew,
　　And all the bugle breezes blew
Reveillée to the breaking morn.

But what is this? I turn about,
　　I find a trouble in thine eye,
　　Which makes me sad, I know not why,
Nor can my dream resolve the doubt:

But ere the lark hath left the lea
　　I wake, and I discern the truth;
　　It is the trouble of my youth
That foolish sleep transfers to thee.

LXVIII.

I DREAM'D there would be Spring no more,
　　That Nature's ancient power was lost:
　　The streets were black with smoke and frost,
They chatter'd trifles at the door:

I wander'd from the noisy town,
　　I found a wood with thorny boughs:
　　I took the thorns to bind my brows,
I wore them like a civic crown:

I met with scoffs, I met with scorns
　　From youth and babe and hoary hairs:
　　They call'd me in the public squares
The fool that wears a crown of thorns:

They call'd me fool, they call'd me child:
  I found an angel of the night;
  The voice was low, the look was bright;
He look'd upon my crown and smiled:

He reach'd the glory of a hand,
  That seem'd to touch it into leaf:
  The voice was not the voice of grief;
The words were hard to understand.

LXIX.

I CANNOT see the features right,
  When on the gloom I strive to paint
  The face I know; the hues are faint
And mix with hollow masks of night;

Cloud-towers by ghostly masons wrought,
  A gulf that ever shuts and gapes,
  A hand that points and palled shapes
In shadowy thoroughfares of thought;

And crowds that stream from yawning doors,
  And shoals of pucker'd faces drive;
  Dark bulks that tumble half alive,
And lazy lengths on boundless shores:

Till all at once beyond the will
  I hear a wizard music roll,
  And thro' a lattice on the soul
Looks thy fair face and makes it still.

LXX.

SLEEP, kinsman thou to death and trance
 And madness, thou hast forged at last
 A night-long Present of the Past
In which we went thro' summer France.

Hadst thou such credit with the soul?
 Then bring an opiate trebly strong,
 Drug down the blindfold sense of wrong
That so my pleasure may be whole;

While now we talk as once we talk'd
 Of men and minds, the dust of change,
 The days that grow to something strange,
In walking as of old we walk'd

Beside the river's wooded reach,
 The fortress, and the mountain ridge,
 The cataract flashing from the bridge,
The breaker breaking on the beach.

LXXI.

RISEST thou thus, dim dawn, again,
 And howlest, issuing out of night,
 With blasts that blow the poplar white,
And lash with storm the streaming pane?

Day, when my crown'd estate begun
 To pine in that reverse of doom,
 Which sicken'd every living bloom,
And blurr'd the splendor of the sun;

Who usherest in the dolorous hour
　With thy quick tears that make the rose
　Pull sideways, and the daisy close
Her crimson fringes to the shower;

Who might'st have heaved a windlass flame
　Up the deep East, or, whispering, play'd
　A chequer-work of beam and shade
Along the hills, yet looked the same,

As wan, as chill, as wild as now;
　Day, mark'd as with some hideous crime
　When the dark hand struck down thro' time,
And cancell'd nature's best: but thou,

Lift as thou mayst thy burthen'd brows
　Thro' clouds that drench the morning star,
　And whirl the ungarner'd sheaf afar,
And sow the sky with flying boughs,

And up thy vault with roaring sound
　Climb thy thick noon, disastrous day;
　Touch thy dull goal of joyless gray,
And hide thy shame beneath the ground.

LXXII.

So many worlds, so much to do,
　So little done, such things to be,
　How know I what had need of thee,
For thou wert strong as thou wert true?

The fame is quench'd that I foresaw,
   The head hath miss'd an earthly wreath:
   I curse not nature, no, nor death;
For nothing is that errs from law.

We pass; the path that each man trod
   Is dim, or will be dim, with weeds:
   What fame is left for human deeds
In endless age? It rests with God.

O hollow wraith of dying fame,
   Fade wholly, while the soul exults,
   And self-infolds the large results
Of force that would have forged a name.

LXXIII.

As sometimes in a dead man's face,
   To those that watch it more and more,
   A likeness, hardly seen before,
Comes out — to some one of his race:

So, dearest, now thy brows are cold,
   I see thee what thou art, and know
   Thy likeness to the wise below,
Thy kindred with the great of old.

But there is more than I can see,
   And what I see I leave unsaid,
   Nor speak it, knowing Death has made
His darkness beautiful with thee.

LXXIV.

I LEAVE thy praises unexpress'd
  In verse that brings myself relief,
  And by the measure of my grief
I leave thy greatness to be guess'd;

What practice howsoe'er expert
  In fitting aptest words to things,
  Or voice the richest-toned that sings,
Hath power to give thee as thou wert?

I care not in these fading days
  To raise a cry that lasts not long,
  And round thee with the breeze of song
To stir a little dust of praise.

Thy leaf has perish'd in the green,
  And, while we breathe beneath the sun,
  The world which credits what is done
Is cold to all that might have been.

So here shall silence guard thy fame;
  But somewhere, out of human view,
  Whate'er thy hands are set to do
Is wrought with tumult of acclaim.

LXXV.

TAKE wings of fancy, and ascend,
  And in a moment set thy face
  Where all the starry heavens of space
Are sharpen'd to a needle's end;

Take wings of foresight; lighten thro'
  The secular abyss to come,
  And lo, thy deepest lays are dumb
Before the mouldering of a yew;

And if the matin songs, that woke
  The darkness of our planet, last,
  Thine own shall wither in the vast,
Ere half the lifetime of an oak.

Ere these have clothed their branchy bowers
  With fifty Mays, thy songs are vain;
  And what are they when these remain
The ruin'd shells of hollow towers?

LXXVI.

WHAT hope is here for modern rhyme
  To him who turns a musing eye
  On songs, and deeds, and lives, that lie
Foreshorten'd in the tract of time?

These mortal lullabies of pain
  May bind a book, may line a box,
  May serve to curl a maiden's locks;
Or when a thousand moons shall wane

A man upon a stall may find,
  And, passing, turn the page that tells
  A grief, then changed to something else,
Sung by a long-forgotten mind.

But what of that? My darken'd ways
　Shall ring with music all the same;
　To breathe my loss is more than fame,
To utter love more sweet than praise.

LXXVII.

AGAIN at Christmas did we weave
　The holly round the Christmas hearth;
　The silent snow possess'd the earth,
And calmly fell our Christmas-eve:

The yule-clog sparkled keen with frost,
　No wing of wind the region swept,
　But over all things brooding slept
The quiet sense of something lost.

As in the winters left behind,
　Again our ancient games had place,
　The mimic picture's breathing grace,
And dance and song and hoodman-blind.

Who show'd a token of distress?
　No single tear, no mark of pain:
　O sorrow, then can sorrow wane?
O grief, can grief be changed to less?

O last regret, regret can die!
　No,—mixt with all this mystic frame,
　Her deep relations are the same,
But with long use her tears are dry.

LXXVIII.

"More than my brothers are to me,"
    Let this not vex thee, noble heart!
    I know thee of what force thou art
To hold the costliest love in fee.

But thou and I are one in kind,
    As moulded like in nature's mint;
    And hill and wood and field did print
The same sweet forms in either mind.

For us the same cold streamlet curl'd
    Thro' all his eddying coves; the same
    All winds that roam the twilight came
In whispers of the beauteous world.

At one dear knee we proffer'd vows,
    One lesson from one book we learn'd,
    Ere childhood's flaxen ringlet turn'd
To black and brown on kindred brows.

And so my wealth resembles thine,
    But he was rich where I was poor,
    And he supplied my wants the more
As his unlikeness fitted mine.

LXXIX.

If any vague desire should rise,
    That holy Death ere Arthur died
    Had moved me kindly from his side,
And dropt the dust on tearless eyes;

Then fancy shapes, as fancy can,
   The grief my loss in him had wrought,
   A grief as deep as life or thought,
But stay'd in peace with God and man.

I make a picture in the brain;
   I hear the sentence that he speaks,
   He bears the burthen of the weeks
But turns his burthen into gain.

His credit thus shall set me free;
   And, influence-rich to soothe and save,
   Unused example from the grave
Reach out dead hands to comfort me.

LXXX.

COULD I have said while he was here,
   " My love shall now no further range;
   There cannot come a mellower change,
For now is love mature in ear."

Love, then, had hope of richer store:
   What end is here to my complaint?
   This haunting whisper makes me faint,
" More years had made me love thee more."

But Death returns an answer sweet:
   "My sudden frost was sudden gain,
   And gave all ripeness to the grain
It might have drawn from after-heat."

LXXXI.

I WAGE not my feud with Death
    For changes wrought on form and face;
    No lower life that earth's embrace
May breed with him can fright my faith.

Eternal process moving on,
    From state to state the spirit walks;
    And these are but the shatter'd stalks,
Or ruin'd chrysalis of one.

Nor blame I Death, because he bare
    The use of virtue out of earth:
    I know transplanted human worth
Will bloom to profit, otherwhere.

For this alone on Death I wreak
    The wrath that garners in my heart;
    He put our lives so far apart
We cannot hear each other speak.

LXXXII.

DIP down upon the northern shore,
    O sweet new-year, delaying long:
    Thou doest expectant nature wrong;
Delaying long, delay no more.

What stays thee from the clouded noons,
    Thy sweetness from its proper place?
    Can trouble live with April days,
Or sadness in the summer moons?

Bring orchis, bring the foxglove spire,
  The little speedwell's darling blue,
  Deep tulips dash'd with fiery dew,
Laburnums, dropping-wells of fire.

O thou, new-year, delaying long,
  Delayest the sorrow in my blood,
  That longs to burst a frozen bud,
And flood a fresher throat with song.

LXXXIII.

WHEN I contemplate all alone
  The life that had been thine below,
  And fix my thoughts on all the glow
To which thy crescent would have grown.

I see thee sitting crown'd with good,
  A central warmth diffusing bliss
  In glance and smile, and clasp and kiss,
On all the branches of thy blood;

Thy blood, my friend, and partly mine
  For now the day was drawing on
  When thou shouldst link thy life with one
Of mine own house, and boys of thine

Had babbled "Uncle" on my knee;
  But that remorseless iron hour
  Made cypress of her orange-flower,
Despair of Hope, and earth of thee.

I seem to meet their least desire,
　　To clap their cheeks, to call them **mine**.
　　I see their unborn faces shine
Beside the never-lighted fire.

I see myself an honor'd guest,
　　Thy partner in the flowery walk
　　Of letters, genial table-talk,
Or deep dispute, and graceful jest;

While now thy prosperous labor fills
　　The lips of men with honest praise,
　　And sun by sun the happy days
Descend below the golden hills.

With promise of a morn as fair;
　　And all the train of bounteous hours
　　Conduct by paths of growing powers
To reverence and the silver hair;

Till slowly worn by earthly robe,
　　Her lavish mission richly wrought,
　　Leaving great legacies of thought,
Thy spirit should fail from off the globe;

What time mine own might also flee,
　　As link'd with thine in love and fate,
　　And, hovering o'er the dolorous strait
To the other shore, involved in thee,

Arrive at last the blessed goal
  And He that died in Holy Land
  Would reach us out the shining hand,
And take us as a single soul.

What reed was that on which I leant?
  Ah, backward fancy, wherefore wake
  The old bitterness again, and break
The low beginnings of content?

LXXXIV.

THIS truth came borne with bier and pall,
  I felt it, when I sorrow'd most,
  'Tis better to have loved and lost,
Than never to have loved at all ——

O true in word, and tried in deed,
  Demanding, so to bring relief
  To this which is our common grief,
What kind of life is that I lead;

And whether trust in things above
  Be dimm'd of sorrow or sustain'd;
  And whether love for him have drain'd
My capabilities of love;

Your words have virtue such as draws
  A faithful answer from the breast,
  Thro' light reproaches, half exprest,
And loyal unto kindl*y* laws.

My blood an even tenor kept,
　　Till on mine ear this message falls,
　　That in Vienna's fatal walls
God's finger touch'd him, and he slept.

The great Intelligences fair
　　That range above our mortal state,
　　In circle round the blessed gate,
Received and gave him welcome there;

And led him thro' the blissful climes,
　　And show'd him in the fountain fresh
　　All knowledge that the sons of flesh
Shall gather in the cycled times.

But I remain'd, whose hopes were dim,
　　Whose life, whose thoughts were little worth,
　　To wander on a darken'd earth,
Where all things round me breathed of him.

O friendship, equal-poised control,
　　O heart, with kindliest motion warm,
　　O sacred essence, other form,
O solemn ghost, O crowned soul!

Yet none could better know than I,
　　How much of act at human hands
　　The sense of human will demands
By which we dare to live or die.

Whatever way my days decline,
　　I felt and feel tho' left alone,
　　His being working in mine own,
The footsteps of his life in mine;

A life that all the Muses deck'd
　　With gifts of grace, that might **express**
　　All-comprehensive tenderness,
All-subtilizing intellect:

And so my passion hath not swerved
　　To works of weakness, but I find
　　An image comforting the mind,
And in my grief a strength reserved.

Likewise the imaginative woe,
　　That loved to handle spiritual **strife**,
　　Diffused the shock thro' all my life,
But in the present broke the blow.

My pulses therefore beat again
　　For other friends that once I met;
　　Nor can it suit me to forget
The mighty hope that makes us **men**.

I woo your love: I count it crime
　　To mourn for any overmuch;
　　I, the divided half of such
A friendship as had master'd Time;

Which masters Time indeed, and is
  Eternal, separate from fears;
  The all-assuming months and years
Can take no part away from this:

But Summer on the steaming floods,
  And Spring that swells the narrow brooks,
  And Autumn, with a noise of rooks,
That gather in the waning woods,

And every pulse of wind and wave
  Recalls, in change of light or gloom,
  My old affection of the tomb,
And my prime passion in the grave:

My old affection of the tomb,
  A part of stillness, yearns to speak:
  "Arise, and get thee forth and seek
A friendship for the years to come.

"I watch thee from the quiet shore;
  Thy spirit up to mine can reach;
  But in dear words of human speech
We two communicate no more."

And I, "Can clouds of nature stain
  The starry clearness of the free?
  How is it? Canst thou feel for me
Some painless sympathy with pain?"

And lightly does the whisper fall:
  " 'Tis hard for thee to fathom this:
  I triumph in conclusive bliss,
And that serene result of all."

So hold I commerce with the dead;
  Or so methinks the dead would say;
  Or so shall grief with symbols play,
And pining life be fancy-fed.

Now looking to some settled end,
  That these things pass, and I shall prove
  A meeting somewhere, love with love,
I crave your pardon, O my friend;

If not so fresh, with love as true,
  I, clasping brother-hands, aver
  I could not, if I would, transfer
The whole I felt for him to you.

For which be they that hold apart
  The promise of the golden hours?
  First love, first friendship, equal powers,
That marry with the virgin heart.

Still mine, that cannot but deplore,
  That beats within a lonely place,
  That yet remembers his embrace,
But at his footstep leaps no more,

My heart, tho' widow'd, may not rest
   Quite in the love of what is gone,
   But seeks to beat in time with one
That warms another living breast.

Ah, take the imperfect gift I bring,
   Knowing the primrose yet is dear,
   The primrose of the later year,
As not unlike to that of Spring.

LXXXV.

SWEET after showers, ambrosial air,
   That rollest from the gorgeous gloom
   Of evening over brake and bloom
And meadow, slowly breathing bare

The round of space, and rapt below
   Thro' all the dewy-tassell'd wood,
   And shadowing down the horned flood
In ripples, fan my brows and blow

The fever from my cheek, and sigh
   The full new life that feeds thy breath
   Throughout my frame, till Doubt and **Death,**
Ill brethren let the fancy fly

From belt to belt of crimson seas
   On leagues of odor streaming far,
   To where in yonder orient star
A hundred spirits whisper "Peace."

LXXXVI.

I PAST beside the reverend walls
   In which of old I wore the gown;
   I roved at random thro' the town,
And saw the tumult of the halls;

And heard once more in college fanes
   The storm their high-built organs make,
   And thunder-music, rolling, shake
The prophets blazon'd on the panes;

And caught once more the distant shout,
   The measured pulse of racing oars
   Among the willows; paced the shores
And many a bridge, and all about

The same gray flats again, and felt
   The same, but not the same; and last
   Up that long walk of limes I past
To see the rooms in which he dwelt.

Another name was on the door:
   I linger'd; all within was noise
   Of songs, and clapping hands, and boys
That crash'd the glass and beat the floor;

Where once we held debate, a band
   Of youthful friends, on mind and art,
   And labor, and the changing mart,
And all the framework of the land;

When one would aim an arrow fair,
　　But send it slackly from the string;
　　And one would pierce an outer ring,
And one an inner, here and there;

And last the master-bowman, he
　　Would cleave the mark.　A willing ear
　　We lent him.　Who, but hung to hear
The rapt oration flowing free

From point to point, with power and grace
　　And music in the bounds of law,
　　To those conclusions when we saw
The God within him light his face,

And seem to lift the form, and glow
　　In azure orbits heavenly-wise;
　　And over those ethereal eyes
The bar of Michael Angelo.

LXXXVII.

WILD bird, whose warble, liquid sweet,
　　Rings Eden thro' the budded quicks,
　　O tell me where the senses mix,
O tell me where the passions meet,

Whence radiate: fierce extremes employ
　　Thy spirits in the darkening leaf,
　　And in the midmost heart of grief
Thy passion clasps a secret joy:

And I — my harp would prelude woe —
　I cannot all command the strings:
　The glory of the sum of things
Will flash along the chords and go.

LXXXVIII.

WITCH-ELMS that counterchange the floor
　Of this flat lawn with dusk and bright;
　And thou, with all thy breadth and height
Of foliage, towering sycamore;

How often, hither wandering down,
　My Arthur found your shadows fair,
　And shook to all the liberal air
The dust and din and steam of town:

He brought an eye for all he saw;
　He mixt in all our simple sports;
　They pleased him, fresh from broiling courts
And dusty purlieus of the law.

O joy to him in this retreat,
　Immantled in ambrosial dark,
　To drink the cooler air, and mark
The landscape winking thro' the heat.

O sound to rout the brood of cares,
　The sweep of scythe in morning dew,
　The gust that round the garden flew,
And tumbled half the mellowing pears!

O bliss, when all in circle drawn
  About him, heart and ear were fed
  To hear him, as he lay and read
The Tuscan poet on the lawn:

Or in the all-golden afternoon
  A guest, or happy sister, sung,
  Or here she brought the harp and flung
A ballad to the brightening moon:

Nor less it pleased in livelier moods,
  Beyond the bounding hill to stray,
  And break the livelong summer day
With banquet in the distant woods;

Whereat we glanced from theme to theme,
  Discuss'd the books to love or hate,
  Or touch'd the changes of the state,
Or threaded some Socratic dream;

But if I praised the busy town,
  He loved to rail against it still,
  For " ground in yonder social mill,
We rub each other's angles down,

" And merge," he said, " in form and gloss
  The picturesque of man and man."
  We talk'd: the stream beneath us ran,
The wine-flask lying couch'd in moss,

Or cool'd within the glooming wave;
  And last, returning from afar,
  Before the crimson-circled star
Had fall'n into her father's grave,

And brushing ankle-deep in flowers,
  We heard behind the woodbine veil
  The milk that bubbled in the pail,
And buzzings of the honeyed hours.

LXXXIX.

HE tasted love with half his mind,
  Nor ever drank the inviolate spring
  Where nighest heaven, who first could fling
This bitter seed among mankind:

That could the dead, whose dying eyes
  Were closed with wail, resume their life,
  They would but find in child and wife
An iron welcome when they rise:

'T was well, indeed, when warm with wine,
  To pledge them with a kindly tear,
  To talk them o'er, to wish them here,
To count their memories half divine;

But if they came who passed away,
  Behold their brides in other hands;
  The hard heir strides about their lands,
And will not yield them for a day.

Yea, tho' their sons were none of these,
　　Not less the yet-loved sire would make
　　Confusion worse than death, and shake
The pillars of domestic peace.

Ah dear, but come thou back to me:
　　Whatever change the years have wrought
　　I find not yet one lonely thought
That cries against my wish for thee.

XC.

WHEN rosy plumelets tuft the larch,
　　And rarely pipes the mounted thrush;
　　Or underneath the barren bush
Flits by the sea-blue bird of March;

Come, wear the form by which I know
　　Thy spirit in time among thy peers;
　　The hope of unaccomplish'd years
Be large and lucid round thy brow.

When summer's hourly-mellowing change
　　May breathe, with many roses sweet,
　　Upon the thousand waves of wheat,
That ripple round the lonely grange;

Come: not in watches of the night,
　　But where the sunbeam broodeth warm,
　　Come, beauteous in thine after form,
And like a finer light in light.

XCI.

IF any vision should reveal
   Thy likeness, I might count it vain,
   As but the canker of the brain;
Yea, tho' it spake and made appeal

To chances where our lots were cast
   Together in the days behind.
   I might but say, I hear a wind
Of memory murmuring the past.

Yea, tho' it spake and bared to view
   A fact within the coming year;
   And tho' the months, revolving near,
Should prove the phantom-warning true,

They might not seem thy prophecies,
   But spiritual presentiments,
   And such refraction of events
As often rises ere they rise.

XCII.

I SHALL not see thee.   Dare I say
   No spirit ever brake the band
   That stays him from the native land,
Where first he walk'd when claspt in clay?

No visual shade of some one lost,
   But he, the Spirit himself, may come
   Where all the nerve of sense is numb;
Spirit to Spirit, Ghost to Ghost.

O, therefore from thy sightless range
  With gods in unconjectured bliss,
  O, from the distance of the abyss
Of tenfold-complicated change,

Descend, and touch, and enter; hear
  The wish too strong for words to name;
  That in this blindness of the frame
My Ghost may feel that thine is near.

XCIII.

How pure at heart and sound in head,
  With what divine affections bold,
  Should be the man whose thought would hold
An hour's communion with the dead.

In vain shalt thou, or any, call
  The spirits from their golden day,
  Except, like them, thou too canst say,
My spirit is at peace with all.

They haunt the silence of the breast,
  Imaginations calm and fair,
  The memory like a cloudless air,
The conscience as a sea at rest.

But when the heart is full of din,
  And doubt beside the portal waits,
  They can but listen at the gates,
And hear the household jar within.

XCIV.

By night we linger'd on the lawn,
  For underfoot the herb was dry;
  And genial warmth; and o'er the sky
The silvery haze of summer drawn;

And calm that let the tapers burn
  Unwavering: not a cricket chirr'd:
  The brook alone far-off was heard,
And on the board the fluttering urn:

And bats went round in fragrant skies,
  And wheel'd or lit the filmy shapes
  That haunt the dusk, with ermine capes
And woolly breasts and beaded eyes;

While now we sang old songs that peal'd
  From knoll to knoll, where, couch'd at ease,
  The white kine glimmer'd, and the trees
Laid their dark arms about the field.

But when those others, one by one,
  Withdrew themselves from me and night,
  And in the house light after light
Went out, and I was all alone,

A hunger seized my heart; I read
  Of that glad year that once had been,
  In those fall'n leaves which kept their green,
The noble letters of the dead:

And strangely on the silence broke
   The silent-speaking words, and strange
   Was love's dumb cry defying change
To test his worth; and strangely spoke

The faith, the vigor, bold to dwell
   On doubts that drive the coward back,
   And keen thro' wordy snares to track
Suggestion to her inmost cell.

So word by word, and line by line,
   The dead man touch'd me from the past,
   And all at once it seem'd at last
His living soul was flash'd on mine,

And mine in his was wound, and whirl'd
   About empyreal heights of thought,
   And came on that which is, and caught
The deep pulsations of the world,

Æonian music measuring out
   The steps of Time, the shocks of Chance,
   The blows of Death. At length my trance
Was cancell'd, stricken thro' with doubt.

Vague words! but ah, how hard to frame
   In matter-moulded forms of speech,
   Or ev'n for intellect to reach
Thro' memory that which I became:

Till now the doubtful dusk reveal'd
　　The knoll once more where, couch'd at ease,
　　The white kine glimmer'd, and the trees
Laid their dark arms about the field:

And suck'd from out the distant gloom,
　　A breeze began to tremble o'er
　　The large leaves of the sycamore,
And fluctuate all the still perfume,

And gathering freshlier overhead,
　　Rock'd the full-foliaged elms, and swung
　　The heavy-folded rose, and flung
The lilies to and fro, and said,

"The dawn, the dawn," and died away;
　　And East and West, without a breath,
　　Mixt their dim lights, like life and death,
To broaden into boundless day.

XCV.

You say, but with no touch of scorn,
　　Sweet-hearted, you, whose light-blue eyes
　　Are tender over drowning flies,
You tell me, doubt is Devil-born.

I know not: one indeed I knew
　　In many a subtle question versed,
　　Who touch'd a jarring lyre at first,
But ever strove to make it true:

Perplext in faith, but pure in deeds,
   At last he beat his music out.
   There lives more faith in honest doubt,
Believe me, than in half the creeds.

He fought his doubts and gather'd strength,
   He would not make his judgment blind,
   He faced the spectres of the mind
And laid them: thus he came at length

To find a stronger faith his own;
   And Power was with him in the night,
   Which makes the darkness and the light,
And dwells not in the light alone,

But in the darkness and the cloud,
   As over Sinai's peaks of old,
   While Israel made their gods of gold,
Altho' the trumpet blew so loud.

XCVI.

My love has talk'd with rocks and trees;
   He finds on misty mountain-ground
   His own vast shadow glory-crown'd;
He sees himself in all he sees.

Two partners of a married life,—
   I look'd on these, and thought of thee
   In vastness and in mystery,
And of my spirit as of a wife.

These two — they dwelt with eye on eye,
  Their hearts of old have beat in tune,
  Their meetings made December June,
Their every parting was to die.

Their love has never past away;
  The days she never can forget
  Are earnest that he loves her yet,
Whate'er the faithless people say.

Her life is lone, he sits apart,
  He loves her yet, she will not weep,
  Tho' rapt in matters dark and deep
He seems to slight her simple heart.

He thrids the labyrinth of the mind,
  He reads the secret of the star,
  He seems so near and yet so far,
He looks so cold: she thinks him kind.

She keeps the gift of years before,
  A wither'd violet is her bliss:
  She knows not what his greatness is
For that, for all, she loves him more.

For him she plays, to him she sings
  Of early faith and plighted vows;
  She knows but matters of the house,
And he, he knows a thousand things.

Her faith is fixt and cannot move,
    She darkly feels him great and wise,
    She dwells on him with faithful eyes,
"I cannot understand: I love."

XCVII.

You leave us: you will see the Rhine,
    And those fair hills I sail'd below,
    When I was there with him; and go
By summer belts of wheat and vine

To where he breathed his latest breath,
    That City.   All her splendor seems
    No livelier than the wisp that gleams
On Lethe in the eyes of Death.

Let her great Danube rolling fair
    Enwind her isles, unmark'd of me;
    I have not seen, I will not see
Vienna; rather dream that there,

A treble darkness, Evil haunts
    The birth, the bridal; friend from friend
    Is oftener parted, fathers bend
Above more graves, a thousand wants

Gnarr at the heels of men, and prey
    By each cold hearth, and sadness flings
    Her shadow on the blaze of kings:
And yet myself have heard him say,

That not in any mother town
   With statelier progress to and fro
   The double tides of chariots flow
By park and suburb under brown

Of lustier leaves; nor more content,
   He told me, lives in any crowd,
   When all is gay with lamps, and loud
With sport and song, in booth and tent,

Imperial halls, or open plain;
   And wheels the circled dance, and breaks
   The rocket molten into flakes
Of crimson or in emerald rain.

XCVIII.

RISEST thou thus, dim dawn, again,
   So loud with voices of the birds,
   So thick with lowings of the herds,
Day, when I lost the flower of men;

Who tremblest thro' thy darkling red
   On yon swoll'n brook that bubbles fast
   By meadows breathing of the past,
And woodlands holy to the dead;

Who murmurest in the foliaged eaves
   A song that slights the coming care,
   And Autumn laying here and there
A fiery finger on the leaves;

Who wakenest with thy balmy breath,
　　To myriads on the genial earth,
　　Memories of bridal, or of birth,
And unto myriads more of death.

O, wheresoever those may be,
　　Betwixt the slumber of the poles,
　　To-day they come as kindred souls;
They know me not, but mourn with me.

XCIX.

I CLIMB the hill: from end to end
　　Of all the landscape underneath,
　　I find no place that does not breathe
Some gracious memory of my friend;

No gray old grange, or lonely fold,
　　Or low morass and whispering reed,
　　Or simple stile from mead to mead,
Or sheepwalk up the windy wold;

No hoary knoll of ash and haw
　　That hears the latest linnet trill,
　　Nor quarry trench'd along the hill,
And haunted by the wrangling daw;

Nor runlet tinkling from the rock:
　　Nor pastoral rivulet that swerves
　　To left and right thro' meadowy curves,
That feed the mothers of the flock;

But each has pleased a kindred eye,
  And each reflects a kindlier day;
  And, leaving these, to pass away,
I think once more he seems to die.

C.

UNWATCH'D, the garden bough shall sway,
  The tender blossom flutter down,
  Unloved, that beach will gather brown,
This maple burn itself away;

Unloved, the sun-flower, shining fair,
  Ray round with flames her disk of seed,
  And many a rose-carnation feed
With summer spice the humming air;

Unloved, by many a sandy bar,
  The brook shall babble down the plain,
  At noon, or when the lesser wain
Is twisting round the polar star;

Uncared for, gird the windy grove,
  And flood the haunts of hern and crake;
  Or into silver arrows break
The sailing moon in creek and cove;

Till from the garden and the wild
  A fresh association blow,
  And year by year the landscape grow,
Familiar to the stranger's child;

As year by year the laborer tills
　　His wonted glebe, or lops the glades;
　　And year by year our memory fades
From all the circle of the hills.

CI.

WE leave the well-beloved place
　　Where first we gazed upon the sky;
　　The roofs, that heard our earliest cry,
Will shelter one of stranger race.

We go, but ere we go from home,
　　As down the garden-walks I move,
　　Two spirits of a diverse love
Contend for loving masterdom.

One whispers, thy boyhood sung
　　Long since its matin song, and heard
　　The low love-language of the bird
In native hazels tassel-hung.

The other answers, " Yea, but here
　　Thy feet have strayed in after hours
　　With thy lost friend among the bowers,
And this hath made them trebly dear."

These two have striven half the day,
　　And each prefers his separate claim
　　Poor rivals in a losing game,
That will not yield each other way.

I turn to go : my feet are set
　　To leave the pleasant fields and farms ;
　　They mix in one another's arms
To one pure image of regret.

CII.

On that last night before we went
　　From out the doors where I was bred,
　　I dream'd a vision of the dead,
Which left my after-morn content.

Methought I dwelt within a hall,
　　And maidens with me : distant hills
　　From hidden summits fed with rills
A river sliding by the wall.

The hall with harp and carol rang.
　　They sang of what is wise and good
　　And graceful.　In the centre stood
A statue veil'd, to which they sang ;

And which tho' veil'd was known to me,
　　The shape of him I loved, and love
　　Forever : then flew in a dove
And brought a summons from the sea ;

And when they learnt that I must go,
　　They wept and wail'd, but led the way
　　To where a little shallop lay
At anchor in the flood below ;

And on by many a level mead,
    And shadowing bluff that made the banks,
    We glided winding under ranks
Of iris, and the golden reed;

And still as vaster grew the shore,
    And roll'd the floods in grander space,
    The maidens gather'd strength and grace
And presence, lordlier than before;

And I myself, who sat apart
    And watch'd them, wax'd in every limb;
    I felt the thews of Anakim,
The pulses of a Titan's heart;

As one would sing the death of war,
    And one would chant the history
    Of that great race which is to be,
And one the shaping of a star;

Until the forward-creeping tides
    Began to foam, and we to draw,
    From deep to deep, to where we saw
A great ship lift her shining sides.

The man we loved was there on deck,
    But thrice as large as man he bent
    To greet us.   Up the side I went,
And fell in silence on his neck:

Whereat those maidens with one mind
 Bewail'd their lot; I did them wrong:
 "We served thee here," they said, "so long,
And wilt thou leave us now behind?"

So rapt I was, they could not win
 An answer from my lips, but he
 Replying, "Enter likewise ye
And go with us:" they enter'd in.

And while the wind began to sweep
 A music out of sheet and shroud,
 We steer'd her toward a crimson cloud
That landlike slept along the deep.

CIII.

THE time draws near the birth of Christ:
 The moon is hid, the night is still;
 A single church below the hill
Is pealing, folded in the mist.

A single peal of bells below,
 That wakens at this hour of rest
 A single murmur in the breast,
That these are not the bells I know.

Like strangers' voices here they sound,
 In lands where not a memory strays,
 Nor landmark breathes of other days,
But all is new unhallow'd ground.

CIV.

THIS holly by the cottage-eave,
　　To-night, ungather'd, shall it stand:
　　We live within the stranger's land,
And strangely falls our Christmas-eve.

Our father's dust is left alone
　　And silent under other snows:
　　There in due time the woodbine blows,
The violet comes, but we are gone.

No more shall wayward grief abuse
　　The genial hour with mask and mime;
　　For change of place, like growth of time,
Has broke the bond of dying use.

Let cares that petty shadows cast,
　　By which our lives are chiefly proved,
　　A little spare the night I loved,
And hold it solemn to the past.

But let no footstep beat the floor,
　　Nor bowl of wassail mantel warm;
　　For who would keep an ancient form
Thro' which the spirit breathes no more?

Be neither song, nor game, nor feast;
　　Nor harp be touch'd, nor flute be blown;
　　No dance, no motion, save alone
What lightens in the lucid east

Of rising worlds by yonder wood.
    Long sleeps the summer in the seed;
    Run out your measured arcs, and lead
The closing cycle rich in good.

CV.

RING out wild bells to the wild sky,
    Thy flying cloud, the frosty light:
    The year is dying in the night;
Ring out, wild bells, and let him die.

Ring out the old, ring in the new,
    Ring, happy bells, across the snow:
    The year is going, let him go;
Ring out the false, ring in the true.

Ring out the grief that saps the mind,
    For those that here we see no more;
    Ring out the feud of rich and poor,
Ring in redress to all mankind.

Ring out a slowly dying cause,
    And ancient forms of party strife;
    Ring in the nobler modes of life,
With sweeter manners, purer laws.

Ring out the want, the care, the sin,
    The faithless coldness of the times;
    Ring out, ring out my mournful rhymes,
But ring the fuller minstrel in.

Ring out false pride in place and blood,
  The civic slander and the spite;
  Ring in the love of truth and right,
Ring in the common love of good.

Ring out old shapes of foul disease;
  Ring out the narrowing lust of gold;
  Ring out the thousand wars of old,
Ring in the thousand years of peace.

Ring in the valiant man and free,
  The larger heart, the kindlier hand;
  Ring out the darkness of the land,
Ring in the Christ that is to be.

CVI.

It is the day when he was born,
  A bitter day that early sank
  Behind a purple-frosty bank
Of vapor, leaving night forlorn.

The time admits not flowers or leaves
  To deck the banquet.   Fiercely flies
  The blast of North and East, and ice
Makes daggers at the sharpen'd eaves,

And bristles all the brakes and thorns
  To yon hard crescent, as she hangs
  Above the wood which grides and clangs
Its leafless ribs and iron horns

Together, in the drifts that pass
  To darken on the rolling brine
  That breaks the coast.   But fetch the wine,
Arrange the board and brim the glass;

Bring in great logs and let them lie,
  To make a solid core of heat;
  Be cheerful-minded, talk and treat
Of all things ev'n as he were by;

We keep the day.   With festal cheer,
  With books and music, surely we
  Will drink to him whate'er he be,
And sing the songs he loved to hear.

CVII.

I WILL not shut me from my kind,
  And, lest I stiffen into stone,
  I will not eat my heart alone,
Nor feed with sighs a passing wind:

What profit lies in barren faith,
  And vacant yearning, tho' with might
  To scale the heaven's highest height,
Or dive below the wells of Death?

What find I in the highest place,
  But mine own phantom chanting hymns?
  And on the depths of death there swims
The reflex of a human face.

I'll rather take what fruit may be
 Of sorrow under human skies;
 'T is held that sorrow makes us wise,
Whatever wisdom sleep with thee.

CVIII.

HEART-AFFLUENCE in discursive talk
 From household fountains never dry;
 The critic clearness of an eye,
That saw thro' all the Muses' walk;

Seraphic intellect and force
 To seize and throw the doubts of man;
 Impassion'd logic, which outran
The hearer in its fiery course;

High nature amorous of the good,
 But touch'd with no ascetic gloom;
 And passion pure in snowy bloom
Thro' all the years of April blood;

A love of freedom rarely felt,
 Of freedom in her regal seat
 Of England; not the school-boy heat,
The blind hysterics of the Celt;

And manhood fused with female grace
 In such a sort, the child would twine
 A trustful hand, unask'd, in thine,
And find his comfort in thy face;

All these have been, and thee mine eyes
  Have look'd on: if they look'd in vain,
  My shame is greater who remain,
Nor let thy wisdom make me wise.

CIX.

THY converse drew us with delight,
  The men of rathe and riper years:
  The feeble soul, a haunt of fears,
Forgot his weakness in thy sight.

On thee the loyal-hearted hung,
  The proud was half disarm'd of pride,
  Nor cared the serpent at thy side
To flicker with his double tongue.

The stern were mild when thou wert by,
  The flippant put himself to school
  And heard thee, and the brazen fool
Was soften'd, and he knew not why;

While I, thy dearest, sat apart,
  And felt thy triumph was as mine;
  And loved them more, that they were **thine**,
The graceful tact, the Christian art;

Not mine the sweetness or the skill
  But mine the love that will not tire,
  And, born of love, the vague desire
That spurs an imitative will.

CX.

THE churl in spirit, up or down
   Along the scale of ranks, thro' all,
   To him who grasps a golden ball,
By blood a king, at heart a clown;

The churl in spirit, howe'er he veil
   His want in forms for fashion's sake,
   Will let his coltish nature break
At seasons thro' the gilded pale:

For who can always act? but he,
   To whom a thousand memories call,
   Not being less but more than all
The gentleness he seem'd to be,

Best seem'd the thing he was, and join'd
   Each office of the social hour
   To noble manners, as the flower
And native growth of noble mind;

Nor ever narrowness or spite,
   Or villain fancy fleeting by,
   Drew in the expression of an eye,
Where God and Nature met in light;

And thus he bore without abuse
   The grand old name of gentleman,
   Defamed by every charlatan,
And soil'd with all ignoble use.

CXI.

HIGH wisdom holds my wisdom less,
 That I, who gaze with temperate eyes
 On glorious insufficiencies,
Set light by narrower perfectness.

But thou, that fillest all the room
 Of all my love, art reason why
 I seem to cast a careless eye
On souls, the lesser lords of doom.

For what wert thou? some novel power
 Sprang up forever at a touch,
 And hope could never hope too much,
In watching thee from hour to hour,

Large elements in order brought,
 And tracks of calm from tempest made,
 And world-wide fluctuation sway'd
In vassal tides that follow'd thought.

CXII.

'T IS held that sorrow makes us wise;
 Yet how much wisdom sleeps with thee
 Which not alone had guided me,
But served the seasons that may rise;

For can I doubt who knew thee keen
 In intellect, with force and skill
 To strive, to fashion, to fulfil —
I doubt not what thou wouldst have been:

A life in civic action warm,
   A soul on highest mission sent,
   A potent voice of Parliament,
A pillar steadfast in the storm,

Should licensed boldness gather force,
   Becoming, when the time has birth,
   A lever to uplift the earth
And roll it in another course,

With thousand shocks that come and go,
   With agonies, with energies,
   With overthrowings, and with cries,
And undulations to and fro.

CXIII.

Who loves not Knowledge?   Who shall rail
   Against her beauty? May she mix
   With men and prosper! Who shall fix
Her pillars?   Let her work prevail.

But on her forehead sits a fire:
   She sets her forward countenance
   And leaps into the future chance,
Submitting all things to desire.

Half-grown as yet, a child, and vain,
   She cannot fight the fear of death.
   What is she, cut from love and faith,
But some wild Pallas from the brain

Of Demons? fiery-hot to burst
  All barriers in her onward race
  For power.   Let her know her place;
She is the second, not the first.

A higher hand must make her mild,
  If all be not in vain: and guide
  Her footsteps, moving side by side
With wisdom, like the younger child:

For she is earthly of the mind,
  But Wisdom heavenly of the soul.
  O friend, who camest to thy goal
So early, leaving me behind,

I would the great world grew like thee,
  Who grewest not alone in power
  And knowledge, but by year and hour
In reverence and in charity.

CXIV.

Now fades the last long streak of snow,
  Now bourgeons every maze of quick
  About the flowering squares, and thick
By ashen roots the violets blow.

Now rings the woodland loud and long,
  The distance takes a lovelier hue,
  And drown'd in yonder living blue
The lark becomes a sightless song.

Now dance the lights on lawn and lea,
  The flocks are whiter down the vale,
  And milkier every milky sail
On winding stream or distant sea;

Where now the seamew pipes, or dives
  In yonder gleaming green, and fly
  The happy birds that change their sky
To build and brood; that live their lives

From land to land; and in my breast
  Spring wakens too; and my regret
  Becomes an April violet,
And buds and blossoms like the rest.

CXV.

Is it, then, regret for buried time
  That keenlier in sweet April wakes,
  And meets the year, and gives and takes
The colors of the crescent prime?

Not all: the songs, the stirring air,
  The life re-orient out of dust,
  Cry thro' the sense to hearten trust
In that which made the world so fair.

Not all regret: the face will shine
  Upon me, while I muse alone;
  And that dear voice I once have known
Still speak to me of me and mine:

Yet less of sorrow lives in me
  For days of happy commune dead;
  Less yearning for the friendship fled,
Than some strong bond which is to be.

CXVI.

O DAYS and hours, your work is this,
  To hold me from my proper place,
  A little while from his embrace,
For fuller gain of after bliss;

That out of distance might ensue
  Desire of nearness doubly sweet;
  And unto meeting when we meet,
Delight a hundred-fold accrue,

For every grain of sand that runs,
  And every span of shade that steals,
  And every kiss of toothed wheels,
And all the courses of the suns.

CXVII.

CONTEMPLATE all this work of Time,
  The giant laboring in his youth;
  Nor dream of human love and truth,
As dying Nature's earth and lime;

But trust that those we call the dead
  Are breathers of an ampler day,
  Forever nobler ends.   They say,
The solid earth whereon we tread

In tracts of fluent heat began,
   And grew to seeming-random forms,
   The seeming prey of cyclic storms,
Till at the last arose the man;

Who throve and branch'd from clime to **clime**
   The herald of a higher race,
   And of himself in higher place
If so he type this work of time

Within himself, from more to more;
   Or, crown'd with attributes of woe
   Like glories, move his course, and show
That life is not as idle ore,

But iron dug from central gloom,
   And heated hot with burning fears,
   And dipt in baths of hissing tears,
And batter'd with the shocks of doom

To shape and use.   Arise and fly
   The reeling Faun, the sensual feast;
   Move upward, working out the beast,
And let the ape and tiger die.

CXVIII.

Doors, where my heart was used to be**at**
   So quickly, not as one that weeps
   I come once more; the city sleeps;
I smell the meadow in the street;

I hear a chirp of birds; I see
   Betwixt the black fronts long withdrawn
   A light-blue lane of early dawn,
And think of early days and thee,

And bless thee, for thy lips are bland,
   And bright the friendship of thine eye:
   And in my thoughts with scarce a sigh
I take the pressure of thine hand.

CXIX.

I TRUST I have not wasted breath;
   I think we are not wholly brain,
   Magnetic mockeries; not in vain,
Like Paul with beasts, I fought with Death.

Not only cunning casts in clay:
   Let Science prove we are, and then
   What matters Science unto men,
At least to me? I would not stay.

Let him, the wiser man who springs
   Hereafter, up from childhood shape
   His action, like the greater ape,
But I was born to other things.

CXX.

SAD Hesper o'er the buried sun,
   And ready, thou, to die with him,
   Thou watchest all things ever dim
And dimmer, and a glory done:

The team is loosen'd from the wain,
   The boat is drawn upon the shore;
   Thou listenest to the closing door,
And life is darken'd in the brain.

Bright Phosphor, fresher for the night,
   By thee the world's great work is heard
   Beginning, and the wakeful bird:
Behind thee comes the greater light:

The market boat is on the stream,
   And voices hail it from the brink;
   Thou hear'st the village hammer clink,
And see'st the moving of the team.

Sweet Hesper-Phosphor, double name
   For what is one, the first, the last,
   Thou, like my present and my past,
Thy place is changed; thou art the same.

CXXI.

O, WAST thou with me, dearest, then,
   While I rose up against my doom,
   And yearn'd to burst the folded gloom
To bare the eternal Heavens again,

To feel once more, in placid awe,
   The strong imagination roll
   A sphere of stars about my soul,
In all her motion one with law.

If thou wert with me, and the grave
  Divide us not, be with me now,
  And enter in at breast and brow,
Till all my blood, a fuller wave,

Be quickened with a livelier breath,
  And live an inconsiderate boy,
  As in the former flash of joy,
I slip the thoughts of life and death:

And all the breeze of Fancy blows,
  And every dew-drop paints a bow,
  The wizard lightnings deeply glow,
And every thought breaks out a rose.

CXXII.

There rolls the deep where grew the tree.
  O earth, what changes thou hast seen!
  There where the long street roars, hath been
The stillness of the central sea.

The hills are shadows, and they flow
  From form to form, and nothing stands;
  They melt like mist, the solid lands,
Like clouds they shape themselves and go.

But in my spirit will I dwell,
  And dream my dream, and hold it true;
  For tho' my lips may breathe adieu,
I cannot think the thing farewell.

CXXIII.

THAT which we dare invoke to bless;
   Our dearest faith; our ghastliest doubt;
   He, They, One, All; within, without;
The Power in darkness whom we guess;

I found Him not in world or sun,
   Or eagle's wing, or insect's eye:
   Nor thro' the questions men may try,
The petty cobwebs we have spun:

If e'er, when faith had fall'n asleep,
   I heard a voice, " Believe no more,"
   And heard an ever-breaking shore
That tumbled in the Godless deep:

A warmth within the breast would melt
   The freezing reason's colder part,
   And like a man in wrath the heart
Stood up and answer'd, " I have felt."

No, like a child in doubt and fear:
   But that blind clamor made me wise;
   Then was I as a child that cries,
But, crying, knows his father near;

And what I am beheld again
   What is, and no man understands,
   And out of darkness came the hands
That reach thro' nature, moulding men.

CXXIV.

WHATEVER I have said or sung,
  Some bitter notes my harp would give,
  Yea, tho' there often seem'd to live
A contradiction on the tongue,

Yet Hope had never lost her youth:
  She did but look thro' dimmer eyes;
  Or Love but play'd with gracious lies
Because he felt so fix'd in truth:

And if the song were full of care,
  He breathed the spirit of the song;
  And if the words were sweet and strong,
He set his royal signet there;

Abiding with me till I sail
  To seek thee on the mystic deeps,
  And this electric force, that keeps
A thousand pulses dancing, fail.

CXXV.

LOVE is and was my Lord and King,
  And in his presence I attend
To hear the tidings of my friend,
  Which every hour his couriers bring.

Love is and was my King and Lord,
  And will be, tho' as yet I keep
  Within his court on earth, and sleep
Encompass'd by his faithful guard,

And hear at times a sentinel
    Who moves about from place to place,
    And whispers to the worlds of space,
In the deep night, that all is well.

CXXVI.

AND all is well, tho' faith and form
    Be sunder'd in the night of fear:
    Well roars the storm to those that hear
A deeper voice across the storm,

Proclaiming social truth shall spread,
    And justice, ev'n tho' thrice again
    The red fool-fury of the Seine
Should pile her barricades with dead.

But ill for him that wears a crown,
    And him, the lazar, in his rags:
    They tremble, the sustaining crags;
The spires of ice are toppled down,

And molten up, and roar in flood;
    The fortress crashes from on high,
    The brute earth lightens to the sky,
And the great Æon sinks in blood,

And compass'd by the fires of Hell;
    While thou, dear spirit, happy star,
    O'erlook'st the tumult from afar,
And smilest, knowing all is well.

CXXVII.

THE love that rose on stronger wings,
   Unpalsied when we met with Death,
   Is comrade of the lesser faith
That sees the course of human things.

No doubt vast eddies in the flood
   Of onward time shall yet be made,
   And throned races may degrade;
Yet, O ye mysteries of good,

Wild Hours that fly with Hope and Fear,
   If all your office had to do
   With old results that look like new;
If this were all your mission here,

To draw, to sheathe a useless sword,
   To fool the crowd with glorious lies,
   To cleave a creed in sects and cries,
To change the bearing of a word,

To shift an arbitrary power,
   To cramp the student at his desk,
   To make old bareness picturesque
And tuft with grass a feudal tower;

Why then my scorn might well descend
   On you and yours.   I see in part
   That all, as in some piece of art,
Is toil coöperant to an end.

CXXVIII.

DEAR friend, far off, my lost desire,
　So far, so near in woe and weal;
　O loved the most, when most I feel
There is a lower and a higher;

Known and unknown; human, divine;
　Sweet human hand and lips and eye;
　Dear heavenly friend that canst not die,
Mine, mine, forever, ever mine;

Strange friend, past, present, and to be;
　Love deeplier, darklier understood;
　Behold, I dream a dream of good,
And mingle all the world with thee.

CXXIX.

THY voice is on the rolling air;
　I hear thee where the waters run;
　Thou standest in the rising sun,
And in the setting thou art fair.

What art thou then? I cannot guess;
　But tho' I seem in star and flower
　To feel thee some diffusive power,
I do not therefore love thee less:

My love involves the love before;
　My love is vaster passion now;
　Tho' mix'd with God and Nature thou,
I seem to love thee more and more.

Far off thou art, but ever nigh:
    I have thee still, and I rejoice;
    I prosper, circled with thy voice;
I shall not lose thee tho' I die.

CXXX.

O LIVING will that shalt endure
    When all that seems shall suffer shock,
    Rise in the spiritual rock,
Flow thro' our deeds and make them pure,

That we may lift from out of dust
    A voice as unto him that hears,
    A cry above the conquer'd years
To one that with us works, and trusts

With faith that comes of self-control,
    The truths that never can be proved
    Until we close with all we loved,
And all we flow from, soul in soul.

O TRUE and tried, so well and long,
    Demand not thou a marriage lay;
    In that it is thy marriage day
Is music more than any song.

Nor have I felt so much of bliss
    Since first he told me that he loved
    A daughter of our house; nor proved
Since that dark day a day like this;

Tho' I since then have number'd o'er
    Some thrice three years : they went and came,
    Remade the blood and changed the frame,
And yet is love not less, but more ;

No longer caring to embalm
    In dying songs a dead regret,
    But like a statue solid-set,
And moulded in colossal calm.

Regret is dead, but love is more
    Than in the summers that are flown,
    For I myself with these have grown
To something greater than before ;

Which makes appear the songs I made
    As echoes out of weaker times,
    As half but idle brawling rhymes,
The sport of random sun and shade.

But where is she, the bridal flower,
    That must be made a wife ere noon?
    She enters, glowing like the moon
Of Eden on its bridal bower :

On me she bends her blissful eyes,
    And then on thee ; they meet thy look
    And brighten like the star that shook
Betwixt the palms of paradise.

O when her life was yet in bud,
   He too foretold the perfect rose.
   For thee she grew, for thee she grows
Forever, and as fair as good.

And thou art worthy; full of power;
   As gentle; liberal-minded, great,
   Consistent; wearing all that weight
Of learning lightly like a flower.

But now set out: the moon is near,
   And I must give away the bride;
   She fears not, or with thee beside
And me behind her, will not fear:

For I that danced her on my knee,
   That watch'd her on her nurse's arm,
   That shielded all her life from harm,
At last must part with her to thee;

Now waiting to be made a wife,
   Her feet, my darling, on the dead;
   Their pensive tablets round her head,
And the most living words of life

Breathed in her ear. The ring is on,
   The " wilt thou," answer'd, and again
   The " wilt thou " ask'd, till out of twain
Her sweet " I will " has made ye one.

Now sign your names, which shall be read,
   Mute symbols of a joyful morn,
   By village eyes as yet unborn;
The names are sign'd, and overhead

Begins the clash and clang that tells
   The joy to every wandering breeze;
   The blind wall rocks, and on the trees
The dead leaf trembles to the bells.

O happy hour, and happier hours
   Await them.   Many a merry face
   Salutes them — maidens of the place,
That pelt us in the porch with flowers.

O happy hour, behold the bride
   With him to whom her hand I gave.
   They leave the porch, they pass the grave
That has to-day its sunny side.

To-day the grave is bright for me,
   For them the light of life increased,
   Who stay to share the morning feast,
Who rest to-night beside the sea.

Let all my genial spirits advance
   To meet and greet a whiter sun;
   My drooping memory will not shun
The foaming grape of Eastern France.

It circles round, and fancy plays,
   And hearts are warm'd, and faces bloom,
   As drinking health to bride and groom
We wish them store of happy days.

Nor count me all to blame if I
   Conjecture of a stiller guest,
   Perchance, perchance, among the rest,
And, tho' in silence, wishing joy.

But they must go, the time draws on,
   And those white-favor'd horses wait;
   They rise, but linger; it is late;
Farewell, we kiss, and they are gone.

A shade falls on us like the dark
   From little cloudlets on the grass,
   But sweeps away as out we pass
To range the woods, to roam the park,

Discussing how their courtship grew,
   And talk of others that are wed,
   And how she look'd, and what she said,
And back we come at fall of dew.

Again the feast, the speech, the glee,
   The shade of passing thought, the wealth
   Of words and wit, the double health,
The crowning cup, the three-times-three,

And last the dance ; — till I retire :
 Dumb is that tower which spake so loud,
 And high in heaven the streaming cloud,
And on the downs a rising fire ;

And rise, O moon, from yonder down,
 Till over down and over dale
 All night the shining vapor sail
And pass the silent-lighted town,

The white-faced halls, the glancing rills,
 And catch at every mountain head,
 And o'er the friths that branch and spread
Their sleeping silver thro' the hills ;

And touch with shade the bridal doors,
 With tender gloom the roof, the wall ;
 And breaking let the splendor fall
To spangle all the happy shores

By which they rest, and ocean sounds,
 And, star and system rolling past,
 A soul shall draw from out the vast
And strike his being into bounds,

And, moved thro' life of lower phase,
 Result in man, be born and think,
 And act and love, a closer link
Betwixt us and the crowning race

Of those that, eye to eye, shall look
   On knowledge; under whose command
    Is Earth and Earth's, and in their hand
Is Nature like an open book;

No longer half-akin to brute,
   For all we thought and loved and did,
    And hoped, and suffer'd, is but seed
Of what in them is flower and fruit;

Whereof the man, that with me trod
   This planet, was a noble type
    Appearing ere the times were ripe,
That friend of mine who lives in God,

That God, which ever lives and loves,
   One God, one law, one element,
    And one far-off divine event,
To which the whole creation moves.

LOCKSLEY HALL.

COMRADES, leave me here a little, while as yet
    't is early morn;
Leave me here, and when you want me, sound upon
    the bugle horn.

'T is the place, and all around it, as of old, the
    curlews call,
Dreary gleams about the moorland flying over
    Locksley Hall;

Locksley Hall, that in the distance overlooks the
    sandy tracts,
And the hollow ocean-ridges roaring into cataracts.

Many a night from yonder ivied casement, ere I
    went to rest,
Did I look on great Orion sloping slowly to the
    West.

Many a night I saw the Pleiads, rising thro' the
    mellow shade,
Glitter like a swarm of fire-flies tangled in a silver
    braid.

Here about the beach I wander'd, nourishing a
    youth sublime
With the fairy tales of science, and the long result
    of Time;

When the centuries behind me like a fruitful land
    reposed;
When I clung to all the present for the promise that
    it closed:

When I dipt into the future far as human eye could
    see;
Saw the Vision of the world, and all the wonder that
    would be.

In the Spring a fuller crimson comes upon the
    robin's breast;
In the Spring the wanton lapwing gets himself
    another crest;

In the Spring a livelier iris changes on the burnish'd
    dove;
In the Spring a young man's fancy lightly turns to
    thoughts of love.

Then her cheek was pale and thinner than should
    be for one so young,
And her eyes on all my motions with a mute observ-
    ance hung.

And I said, "My cousin Amy, speak, and speak the
    truth to me,

Trust me, cousin, all the current of my being sets
  to thee."

On her pallid cheek and forehead came a color and
  a light,
As I have seen the rosy red flushing in the northern
  night.

And she turn'd — her bosom shaken with a sudden
  storm of sighs —
All the spirit deeply dawning in the dark of hazel
  eyes —

Saying, " I have hid my feelings, fearing they should
  do me wrong ; "
Saying, "Dost thou love me, cousin?" weeping.
  " I have loved thee long."

Love took up the glass of Time, and turn'd it in his
  glowing hands ;
Every moment, lightly shaken, ran itself in golden
  sands.

Love took up the harp of Life, and smote on all the
  chords with might ;
Smote the chord of Self, that, trembling, pass'd in
  music out of sight.

Many a morning on the moorland did we hear the
  copses ring,
And her whisper throng'd my pulses with the
  fulness of the Spring.

Many an evening by the waters did we watch the
    stately ships,
And our spirits rush'd together at the touching of
    the lips.

O my cousin, shallow-hearted! O my Amy, mine
    no more !
O the dreary, dreary moorland! O the barren,
    barren shore!

Falser than all fancy fathoms, falser than all songs
    have sung,
Puppet to a father's threat, and servile to a shrewish
    tongue!

Is it well to wish thee happy? — having known me
    — to decline
On a range of lower feelings and a narrower heart
    than mine !

Yet it shall be: thou shalt lower to his level day
    by day,
What is fine within thee growing coarse to sympa-
    thize with clay.

As the husband is, the wife is: thou art mated with
    a clown,
And the grossness of his nature will have weight to
    drag thee down.

He will hold thee, when his passion shall have spent
    its novel force,

Something better than his dog, a little dearer than
      his horse.

What is this? his eyes are heavy: think not they
      are glazed with wine.
Go to him: it is thy duty: kiss him: take his hand
      in thine.

It may be my lord is weary, that is brain is over-
      wrought;
Soothe him with thy finer fancies, touch him with thy
      lighter thought.

He will answer to the purpose, easy things to under-
      stand —
Better thou wert dead before me, tho' I slew thee
      with my hand!

Better thou and I were lying, hidden from the heart's
      disgrace,
Roll'd in one another's arms, and silent in a last
      embrace.

Cursed be the social wants that sin against the
      strength of youth!
Cursed be the social lies that warp us from the
      living truth!

Cursed be the sickly forms that err from honest
      Nature's rule!
Cursed be the gold that gilds the straiten'd fore-
      head of the fool!

Well —'t is well that I should bluster! — Hadst thou
    less unworthy proved —
Would to God — for I had loved thee more than
    ever wife was loved.

Am I mad, that I should cherish that which bears
    but bitter fruit?
I will pluck it from my bosom, tho' my heart be at
    the root.

Never, tho' my mortal summers to such length of
    years should come
As the many-winter'd crow that leads the clanging
    rookery home.

Where is comfort? in division of the records of the
    mind?
Can I part her from herself, and love her, as I knew
    her, kind?

I remember one that perish'd: sweetly did she
    speak and move:
Such a one do I remember, whom to look at was to
    love.

Can I think of her as dead, and love her for the
    love she bore?
No — she never loved me truly: love is love forever-
    more.

Comfort? comfort scorn'd of devils! this is truth the
    poet sings,

That a sorrow's crown of sorrow is remembering
    happier things.

Drug thy memories, lest thou learn it, lest thy heart
    be put to proof,
In the dead unhappy night, when the rain is on the
    roof.

Like a dog, he hunts in dreams, and thou art staring
    at the wall,
Where the dying night-lamp flickers, and the shad-
    ows rise and fall.

Then a hand shall pass before thee, pointing to his
    drunken sleep,
To thy widow'd marriage pillows, to the tears that
    thou wilt weep.

Thou shalt hear the "Never, never," whisper'd by
    the phantom years,
And a song from out the distance in the ringing of
    thine ears;

And an eye shall vex thee, looking ancient kindness
    on thy pain.
Turn thee, turn thee on thy pillow: get thee to thy
    rest again.

Nay, but Nature brings thee solace: for a tender
    voice will cry.
'T is a purer life than thine; a lip to drain thy trouble
    dry.

Baby lips will laugh me down: my latest rival brings
    thee rest.
Baby fingers, waxen touches, press me from the
    mother's breast.

O, the child too clothes the father with a dearness
    not his due.
Half is thine and half is his: it will be worthy of
    the two.

O, I see thee old and formal, fitted to thy petty
    part,
With a little hoard of maxims preaching down a
    daughter's heart.

"They were dangerous guides the feelings — she
    herself was not exempt —
Truly, she herself had suffer'd" — Perish in thy
    self-contempt!

Overlive it — lower yet — be happy! wherefore
    should I care?
I myself must mix with action, lest I wither by
    despair.

What is that which I should turn to, lighting upon
    days like these?
Every door is barr'd with gold, and opens but to
    golden keys.

Every gate is thronged with suitors, all the markets
    overflow.

I have but an angry fancy: what is that which 1
    should do?

I had been content to perish, falling on the foeman's
    ground,
When the ranks are roll'd in vapor, and the winds
    are laid with sound.

But the jingling of the guinea helps the hurt that
    Honor feels,
And the nations do but murmur, snarling at each
    other's heels.

Can I but relive in sadness? I will turn that earlier
    page.
Hide me from my deep emotion, O thou wondrous
    Mother-Age!

Make me feel the wild pulsation that I felt before
    the strife,
When I heard my days before me, and the tumult
    of my life;

Yearning for the large excitement that the coming
    years would yield,
Eager-hearted as a boy when first he leaves his
    father's field,

And at night along the dusky highway near and
    nearer drawn,
Sees in heaven the light of London flaring like a
    dreary dawn;

And his spirit leaps within him to be gone before
    him then,
Underneath the light he looks at, in among the
    throngs of men;

Men, my brothers, men the workers, ever reaping
    something new:
That which they have done but earnest of the things
    that they shall do:

For I dipt into the future, far as human eye could
    see,
Saw the Vision of the world, and all the wonder
    that would be;

Saw the heavens fill with commerce, argosies of
    magic sails,
Pilots of the purple twilight, dropping down with
    costly bales;

Heard the heavens fill with shouting, and there
    rain'd a ghastly dew
From the nations' airy navies grappling in the cen-
    tral blue;

Far along the world-wide whisper of the south-wind
    rushing warm,
With the standards of the peoples plunging thro'
    the thunder-storm;

Till the war-drum throbb'd no longer, and the
    battle-flags were furl'd

In the Parliament of man, the Federation of the
     world.

There the common sense of most shall hold a fretful
     realm in awe,
And the kindly earth shall slumber, lapt in universal
     law.

So I triumph'd, ere my passion sweeping thro' me
     left me dry,
Left me with the palsied heart, and left me with the
     jaundiced eye;

Eye, to which all order festers, all things here are
     out of joint,
Science moves, but slowly slowly, creeping on from
     point to point:

Slowly comes a hungry people, as a lion, creeping
     nigher,
Glares at one that nods and winks behind a slowly-
     dying fire.

Yet I doubt not thro' the ages one increasing pur-
     pose runs,
And the thoughts of men are widen'd with the
     process of the suns.

What is that to him that reaps not harvest of his
     youthful joys,
Tho' the deep heart of existence beat forever like a
     boy's?

Knowledge comes, but wisdom lingers, and I linger
    on the shore,
And the individual withers, and the world is more
    and more.

Knowledge comes, but wisdom lingers, and he bears
    a laden breast,
Full of sad experience, moving toward the stillness
    of his rest.

Hark, my merry comrades call me, sounding on the
    bugle-horn,
They to whom my foolish passion were a target for
    their scorn:

Shall it not be scorn to me to harp on such a
    moulder'd string?
I am shamed thro' all my nature to have loved so
    slight a thing.

Weakness to be wroth with weakness! woman's
    pleasure, woman's pain —
Nature made them blinder motions bounded in a
    shallower brain:

Woman is the lesser man, and all thy passions,
    match'd with mine,
Are as moonlight unto sunlight, and as water unto
    wine —

Here at least, where nature sickens, nothing. Ah,
    for some retreat

Deep in yonder shining Orient, where my life began
　　　　to beat;

Where in wild Mahratta-battle fell my father evil-
　　　　starr'd; —
I was left a trampled orphan, and a selfish uncle's
　　　　ward.

Or to burst all links of habit — there to wander far
　　　　away,
On from island unto island at the gateways of the
　　　　day.

Larger constellations burning, mellow moons and
　　　　happy skies,
Breadths of tropic shade and palms in cluster, knots
　　　　of Paradise.

Never comes the trader, never floats an European
　　　　flag,
Slides the bird o'er lustrous woodland, swings the
　　　　trailer from the crag;

Droops the heavy-blossom'd bower, hangs the heavy-
　　　　fruited tree —
Summer isles of Eden lying in dark-purple spheres
　　　　of sea.

There methinks would be enjoyment more than in
　　　　this march of mind,
In the steamship, in the railway, in the thoughts
　　　　that shake mankind.

There the passions cramp'd no longer shall have
    scope and breathing-space;
I will take some savage woman, she shall rear my
    dusky race.

Iron-jointed, supple-sinew'd, they shall dive, and
    they shall run,
Catch the wild goat by the hair, and hurl their lances
    in the sun;

Whistle back the parrot's call, and leap the rain-
    bows of the brooks,
Not with blinded eyesight poring over miserable
    books —

Fool, again the dream, the fancy! but I *know* my
    words are wild,
But I count the gray barbarian lower than the
    Christian child.

I, to herd with narrow foreheads, vacant of our
    glorious gains,
Like a beast with lower pleasures, like a beast with
    lower pains!

Mated with a squalid savage — what to me were sun
    or clime?
I the heir of all the ages, in the foremost files of
    time —

I that rather held it better men should perish one
    by one,

Than that earth should stand at gaze like Joshua's
    moon in Ajalon!

Not in vain the distance beacons. Forward, for-
    ward let us range.
Let the great world spin forever down the ringing
    grooves of change.

Thro' the shadow of the globe we sweep into the
    younger day:
Better fifty years of Europe than a cycle of Cathay.

Mother-Age (for mine I knew not) help me as when
    life begun:
Rift the hills, and roll the waters, flash the light-
    nings, weigh the Sun —

O, I see the crescent promise of my spirit hath not
    set.
Ancient founts of inspiration well thro' all my fancy
    yet.

Howsoever these things be, a long farewell to Locks-
    ley Hall!
Now for me the woods may wither, now for me the
    roof-tree fall.

Comes a vapor from the margin, blackening over
    heath and holt,

Cramming all the blast before it, in its breast a
thunderbolt.

Let it fall on Locksley Hall, with rain or hail, or fire
or snow;
For the mighty wind arises, roaring seaward, and I
go.

LOCKSLEY HALL SIXTY YEARS AFTER.

———◦◇◦———

Late, my grandson! half the morning have I paced
these sandy tracts,
Watch'd again the hollow ridges roaring into cata-
racts,

Wander'd back to living boyhood while I heard the
curlews call,
I myself so close on death, and death itself in Locks-
ley Hall.

So — your happy suit was blasted — she the fault-
less, the divine;
And you liken — boyish babble — this boy-love of
yours with mine.

I myself have often babbled doubtless of a foolish
past;
Babble, babble; our old England may go down in
babble at last.

"Curse him!" curse your fellow-victim? call him
dotard in your rage?

Eyes that lured a doting boyhood well might fool a
   dotard's age.

Jilted for a wealthier! wealthier? yet perhaps she
   was not wise ;
I remember how you kiss'd the miniature with those
   sweet eyes.

In the hall there hangs a painting — Amy's arms
   about my neck —
Happy children in a sunbeam sitting on the ribs of
   wreck.

In my life there was a picture, she that clasp'd my
   neck had flown ;
I was left within the shadow sitting on the wreck
   alone.

Yours has been a slighter ailment, will you sicken
   for her sake?
You, not you! your modern amourist is of easier,
   earthlier make.

Amy loved me, Amy fail'd me, Amy was a timid
   child ;
But your Judith — but your worldling — *she* had
   never driven me wild.

She that holds the diamond necklace dearer than
   the golden ring,
She that finds a winter sunset fairer than a morn of
   Spring.

She that in her heart is brooding on his briefer lease
of life,
While she vows "till death shall part us," she the
would-be-widow wife.

She the worldling born of worldlings — father,
mother — be content,
Ev'n the homely farm can teach us there is some-
thing in descent.

Yonder in that chapel, slowly sinking now into the
ground,
Lies the warrior, my forefather, with his feet upon
the hound.

Cross'd! for once he sail'd the sea to crush the
Moslem in his pride;
Dead the warrior, dead his glory, dead the cause in
which he died.

Yet how often I and Amy in the mouldering aisle
have stood,
Gazing for one pensive moment on that founder of
our blood.

There again I stood to-day, and where of old we
knelt in prayer,
Close beneath the casement crimson with the shield
of Locksley — there,

All in white Italian marble, looking still as if she
smiled,

Lies my Amy dead in child-birth, dead the mother,
　　dead the child.

Dead — and sixty years ago, and dead her aged
　　husband now,
I this old white-headed dreamer stoopt and kiss'd
　　her marble brow.

Gone the fires of youth, the follies, furies, curses,
　　passionate tears,
Gone like fires and floods and earthquakes of the
　　planet's dawning years.

Fires that shook me once, but now to silent ashes
　　fall'n away.
Cold upon the dead volcano sleeps the gleam of
　　dying day.

Gone the tyrant of my youth, and mute below the
　　chancel stones,
All his virtues — I forgive them — black in white
　　above his bones.

Gone the comrades of my bivouac, some in fight
　　against the foe,
Some thro' age and slow diseases, gone as all on
　　earth will go.

Gone with whom for forty years my life in golden
　　sequence ran,
She with all the charm of woman, she with all the
　　breadth of man,

Strong in will and rich in wisdom, Edith, loyal,
    lowly, sweet,
Feminine to her inmost heart, and feminine to her
    tender feet,

Very woman of very woman, nurse of ailing body
    and mind,
She that link'd again the broken chain that bound
    me to my kind.

Here to-day was Amy with me, while I wander'd
    down the coast,
Near us Edith's holy shadow, smiling at the slighter
    ghost.

Gone our sailor son thy father, Leonard early lost
    at sea ;
Thou alone, my boy, of Amy's kin and mine art left
    to me.

Gone thy tender-natured mother, wearying to be left
    alone,
Pining for the stronger heart that once had beat
    beside her own.

Truth, for Truth is Truth, he worshipt, being true as
    he was brave ;
Good, for Good is Good, he follow'd, yet he look'd
    beyond the grave,

Wiser there than you, that crowning barren Death
    as lord of all,

Deem this over-tragic drama's closing curtain is the
      pall!

Beautiful was death in him who saw the death but
      kept the deck,
Saving women and their babes, and sinking with
      the sinking wreck,

Gone for ever! Ever? no — for since our dying
      race began,
Ever, ever, and for ever was the leading light of
      man.

Those that in barbarian burials kill'd the slave, and
      slew the wife,
Felt within themselves the sacred passion of the
      second life.

Indian warriors dream of ampler hunting grounds
      beyond the night;
Ev'n the black Australian dying hopes he shall
      return, a white.

Truth for truth, and good for good! The Good,
      the True, the Pure, the Just;
Take the charm "For ever" from them, and they
      crumble into dust.

Gone the cry of "Forward, Forward," lost within a
      growing gloom;
Lost, or only heard in silence from the silence of a
      tomb.

Half the marvels of my morning, triumphs over time
     and space,
Staled by frequence, shrunk by usage into common-
     est commonplace!

"Forward" rang the voices then, and of the many
     mine was one.
Let us hush this cry of "Forward" till ten thousand
     years have gone.

Far among the vanish'd races, old Assyrian kings
     would flay
Captives whom they caught in battle — iron-hearted
     victors they.

Ages after, while in Asia, he that led the wild
     Moguls,
Timur built his ghastly tower of eighty thousand
     human skulls,

Then, and here in Edward's time, an age of noblest
     English names,
Christian conquerors took and flung the conquer'd
     Christian into flames.

Love your enemy, bless your haters, said the Great-
     est of the great;
Christian love among the Churches look'd the twin
     of heathen hate.

From the golden alms of Blessing man had coin'd
     himself a curse:

Rome of Cæsar, Rome of Peter, which was crueller? which was worse?

France had shown a light to all men, preach'd a Gospel, all men's good;
Celtic Demos rose a Demon, shriek'd and slaked the light with blood.

Hope was ever on her mountain, watching till the day begun
Crown'd with sunlight — over darkness — from the still unrisen sun.

Have we grown at last beyond the passions of the primal clan?
"Kill your enemy, for you hate him," still, "your enemy" was a man.

Have we sunk below them? peasants maim the helpless horse, and drive
Innocent cattle under thatch, and burn the kindlier brutes alive.

Brutes, the brutes are not your wrongers — burnt at midnight, found at morn,
Twisted hard in mortal agony with their offspring, born-unborn,

Clinging to the silent Mother! Are we devils? are we men?
Sweet St. Francis of Assisi, would that he were here again,

He that in his Catholic wholeness used to call the
　　　very flowers
Sisters, brothers — and the beasts — whose pains
　　　are hardly less than ours!

Chaos, Cosmos! Cosmos, Chaos! who can tell how
　　　all will end!
Read the wide world's annals, you, and take their
　　　wisdom for your friend.

Hope the best, but hold the Present fatal daughter
　　　of the Past,
Shape your heart to front the hour, but dream not
　　　that the hour will last.

Ay, if dynamite and revolver leave you courage to
　　　be wise:
When was age so cramm'd with menace? madness?
　　　written, spoken lies?

Envy wears the mask of Love, and, laughing sober
　　　fact to scorn,
Cries to Weakest as to Strongest, "Ye are equals,
　　　equal-born."

Equal-born?　O yes, if yonder hill be level with the
　　　flat.
Charm us, Orator, till the Lion look no larger than
　　　the Cat.

Till the Cat thro' that mirage of overheated language
　　　loom

Larger than the Lion, — Demos end in working its
    own doom.

Russia bursts our Indian barrier, shall we fight her?
    shall we yield?
Pause, before you sound the trumpet, hear the voices
    from the field.

Those three hundred millions under one Imperial
    sceptre now,
Shall we hold them? shall we loose them? take the
    suffrage of the plow.

Nay, but these would feel and follow Truth if only
    you and you,
Rivals of realm-ruining party, when you speak were
    wholly true.

Plowmen, Shepherds, have I found, and more than
    once, and still could find,
Sons of God, and kings of men in utter nobleness
    of mind,

Truthful, trustful, looking upward to the practised
    hustings-liar;
So the Higher wields the Lower, while the Lower is
    the Higher.

Here and there a cotter's babe is royal-born by right
    divine;
Here and there my lord is lower than his oxen or
    his swine.

Chaos, Cosmos! Cosmos, Chaos! once again the
      sickening game ;
Freedom, free to slay herself, and dying while they
      shout her name.

Step by step we gain'd a freedom known to Europe,
      known to all ;
Step by step we rose to greatness, — thro' the
      tonguesters we may fall.

You that woo the Voices — tell them " old experi-
      ence is a fool,"
Teach your flatter'd kings that only those who can-
      not read can rule.

Pluck the mighty from their seat, but set no meek
      ones in their place ;
Pillory Wisdom in your markets, pelt your offal at
      her face.

Tumble Nature heel o'er head, and, yelling with the
      yelling street,
Set the feet above the brain and swear the brain is
      in the feet.

Bring the old dark ages back without the faith,
      without the hope,
Break the State, the Church, the Throne, and roll
      their ruins down the slope.

Authors — atheist, essayist, novelist, realist, rhyme-
      ster, play your part,

Paint the mortal shame of nature with the living
hues of Art.

Rip your brothers' vices open, strip your own foul
passions bare;
Down with Reticence, down with Reverence — for-
ward — naked — let them stare.

Feed the budding rose of boyhood with the drain-
age of your sewer;
Send the drain into the fountain, lest the stream
should issue pure.

Set the maiden fancies wallowing in the troughs of
Zolaism, —
Forward, forward, ay and backward, downward too
into the abysm.

Do your best to charm the worst, to lower the rising
race of men;
Have we risen from out the beast, then back into
the beast again?

Only " dust to dust " for me that sicken at your law-
less din,
Dust in wholesome old-world dust before the newer
world begin.

Heated am I? you — you wonder — well, it scarce
becomes mine age —
Patience! let the dying actor mouth his last upon
the stage.

Cries of unprogressive dotage ere the dotard fall
     asleep?
Noises of a current narrowing, not the music of a
     deep?

Ay, for doubtless I am old, and think gray thoughts,
     for I am gray:
After all the stormy changes shall we find a change-
     less May?

After madness, after massacre, Jacobinism and
     Jacquerie,
Some diviner force to guide us thro' the days I shall
     not see?

When the schemes and all the systems, Kingdoms
     and Republics fall,
Something kindlier, higher, holier — all for each
     and each for all?

All the full-brain, half-brain races, led by Justice,
     Love, and Truth;
All the millions one at length, with all the visions
     of my youth?

All diseases quench'd by Science, no man halt, or
     deaf or blind;
Stronger ever born of weaker, lustier body, larger
     mind?

Earth at last a warless world, a single race, a single
     tongue,

I have seen her far away — for is not Earth as yet
    so young? —

Every tiger madness muzzled, every serpent passion
    kill'd,
Every grim ravine a garden, every blazing desert
    till'd,

Robed in universal harvest up to either pole she
    smiles,
Universal ocean softly washing all her warless
    Isles.

Warless? when her tens are thousands, and her
    thousands millions, then —
All her harvest all too narrow — who can fancy
    warless men?

Warless? war will die out late then. Will it ever?
    late or soon?
Can it, till this outworn earth be dead as yon dead
    world the moon?

Dead the new astronomy calls her. . . . On this
    day and at this hour,
In this gap between the sandhills, whence you see
    the Locksley tower,

Here we met, our latest meeting — Amy — sixty
    years ago —
She and I — the moon was falling greenish thro' a
    rosy glow,

Just above the gateway tower, and even where you
      see her now —
Here we stood and claspt each other, swore the
      seeming-deathless vow. . . .

Dead, but how her living glory lights the hall, the
      dune, the grass!
Yet the moonlight is the sunlight, and the sun him-
      self will pass.

Venus near her ! smiling downward at this earthlier
      earth of ours,
Closer on the Sun, perhaps a world of never fading
      flowers.

Hesper, whom the poet call'd the Bringer home of
      all good things.
All good things may move in Hesper, perfect peo-
      ples, perfect kings.

Hesper — Venus — were we native to that splendor
      or in Mars,
We should see the Globe we groan in, fairest of
      their evening stars.

Could we dream of wars and carnage, craft and mad-
      ness, lust and spite,
Roaring London, raving Paris, in that point of peace-
      ful light?

Might we not in glancing heavenward on a star so
      silver-fair,

Yearn, and clasp the hands and murmur, " Would
to God that we were there " ?

Forward, backward, backward, forward, in the im-
measurable sea,
Sway'd by vaster ebbs and flows than can be known
to you or me.

All the suns — are these but symbols of innumerable
man,
Man or Mind that sees a shadow of the planner or
the plan?

Is there evil but on earth? or pain in every peopled
sphere?
Well be grateful for the sounding watchword, " Evo-
lution " here.

Evolution ever climbing after some ideal good,
And Reversion ever dragging Evolution in the
mud.

What are men that He should heed us? cried the
king of sacred song;
Insects of an hour, that hourly work their brother
insect wrong,

While the silent Heavens roll, and Suns along their
fiery way,
All their planets whirling round them, flash a million
miles a day.

Many an Æon moulded earth before her highest,
    man, was born,
Many an Æon too may pass when earth is manless
    and forlorn,

Earth so huge, and yet so bounded — pools of salt,
    and plots of land —
Shallow skin of green and azure — chains of moun-
    tain, grains of sand!

Only That which made us, meant us to be mightier
    by and by,
Set the sphere of all the boundless Heavens within
    the human eye,

Sent the shadow of Himself, the boundless, thro'
    the human soul,
Boundless inward, in the atom, boundless outward,
    in the Whole.

    *   *   *   *   *   *

Here is Locksley Hall, my grandson, here the lion-
    guarded gate.
Not to-night in Locksley Hall — to-morrow — you,
    you come so late.

Wreck'd — your train — or all but wreck'd? a shat-
    ter'd wheel? a vicious boy!
Good, this forward, you that preach it, is it well to
    wish you joy?

Is it well that while we range with Science, glorying
    in the Time,

City children soak and blacken soul and sense in
    city slime?

There among the glooming alleys Progress halts on
    palsied feet,
Crime and hunger cast our maidens by the thousand
    on the street.

There the Master scrimps his haggard sempstress
    of her daily bread,
There a single sordid attic holds the living and the
    dead.

There the smouldering fire of fever creeps across
    the rotted floor,
And the crowded couch of incest in the warrens of
    the poor.

Nay, your pardon, cry your "forward," yours are
    hope and youth, but I —
Eighty winters leave the dog too lame to follow
    with the cry,

Lame and old, and past his time, and passing now
    into the night;
Yet I would the rising race were half as eager for
    the light.

Light the fading gleam of Even? light the glimmer
    of the dawn?
Aged eyes may take the growing glimmer for the
    gleam withdrawn.

Far away beyond her myriad coming changes earth
    will be
Something other than the wildest modern guess of
    you and me.

Earth may reach her earthly-worst, or if she gain
    her earthly-best,
Would she find her human offspring this ideal man
    at rest?

Forward then, but still remember how the course of
    Time will swerve,
Crook and turn upon itself in many a backward
    streaming curve.

Not the Hall to-night, my grandson! Death and
    Silence hold their own.
Leave the Master in the first dark hour of his last
    sleep alone.

Worthier soul was he than I am, sound and honest,
    rustic Squire,
Kindly landlord, boon companion — youthful jeal-
    ousy is a liar.

Cast the poison from your bosom, oust the madness
    from your brain.
Let the trampled serpent show you that you have
    not lived in vain.

Youthful! youth and age are scholars yet but in the
    lower school,

Nor is he the wisest man who never proved himself
    a fool.

Yonder lies our young sea-village — Art and Grace
    are less and less :
Science grows and Beauty dwindles — roofs of slated
    hideousness!

There is one old Hostel left us where they swing
    the Locksley shield,
Till the peasant cow shall butt the " Lion passant "
    from his field.

Poor old Heraldry, poor old History, poor old
    Poetry, passing hence,
In the common deluge drowning old political com-
    mon-sense!

Poor old voice of eighty crying after voices that
    have fled!
All I loved are vanish'd voices, all my steps are on
    the dead.

All the world is ghost to me, and as the phantom
    disappears,
Forward far and far from here is all the hope of
    eighty years.

    *   *   *   *   *   *

In this Hostel — I remember — I repent it o'er his
    grave —
Like a clown — by chance he met me — I refused
    the hand he gave.

From that casement where the trailer mantles all
    the mouldering bricks —
I was then in early boyhood, Edith but a child of
    six —

While I shelter'd in this archway from a day of driv-
    ing showers —
Peept the winsome face of Edith like a flower
    among the flowers.

Here to-night! the Hall to-morrow, when they toll
    the Chapel bell!
Shall I hear in one dark room a wailing, "I have
    loved thee well."

Then a peal that shakes the portal — one has come
    to claim his bride,
Her that shrank, and put me from her, shriek'd, and
    started from my side —

Silent echoes! you, my Leonard, use and not abuse
    your day,
Move among your people, know them, follow him
    who led the way,

Strove for sixty widow'd years to help his homelier
    brother men,
Served the poor, and built the cottage, raised the
    school, and drain'd the fen.

Hears he now the Voice that wrong'd him? who
    shall swear it cannot be?

Earth would never touch her worst, were one in
    fifty such as he.

Ere she gain her Heavenly-best, a God must min-
    gle with the game:
Nay, there may be those about us whom we neither
    see nor name,

Felt within us as ourselves, the Powers of Good,
    the Powers of Ill,
Strowing balm, or shedding poison in the fountains
    of the Will.

Follow you the Star that lights a desert pathway,
    yours or mine.
Forward, till you see the highest Human Nature is
    divine.

Follow Light, and do the Right — for man can half-
    control his doom —
Till you find the deathless Angel seated in the
    vacant tomb.

Forward, let the stormy moment fly and mingle
    with the Past.
I that loathed, have come to love him. Love will
    conquer at the last.

Gone at eighty, mine own age, and I and you will
    bear the pall;
Then I leave thee Lord and Master, latest Lord of
    Locksley Hall.

MAUD.

I.

1.

I HATE the dreadful hollow behind the little wood,
Its lips in the field above are dabbled with blood-
    red heath,
The red ribb'd ledges drip with a silent horror of
    blood,
And Echo there, whatever is ask'd her, answers
    "Death."

2.

For there in the ghastly pit long since a body was
    found,
His who had given me life — O father! O God! was
    it well? —
Mangled, and flatten'd, and crush'd, and dinted into
    the ground
There yet lies the rock that fell with him when he
    fell.

3.

Did he fling himself down? who knows? for a vast
    speculation had fail'd
And ever he mutter'd and madden'd, and ever wann'd
    with despair,

And out he walk'd when the wind like a broken
    worldling wail'd,

And the flying gold of the ruin'd woodlands drove
    thro' the air.

4.

I remember the time, for the roots of my hair were
    stirr'd

By a shuffled step, by a dead weight trail'd, by a
    whisper'd fright,

And my pulses closed their gates with a shock on
    my heart as I heard

The shrill-edged shriek of a mother divide the shud-
    dering night.

5.

Villany somewhere! whose? One says, we are
    villains all.

Not he: his honest fame should at least by me be
    maintain'd:

But that old man, now lord of the broad estate and
    the Hall,

Dropt off gorged from a scheme that had left us
    flaccid and drain'd.

6.

Why do they prate of the blessings of Peace? we
    have made them a curse,

Pickpockets, each hand lusting for all that is not its
    own;

And lust of gain, in the spirit of Cain, is it better or
     worse
Than the heart of the citizen hissing in war on his
     own hearthstone?

7.

But these are the days of advance, the works of the
     men of mind,
When who but a fool would have faith in a trades-
     man's ware or his word?
Is it peace or war?   Civil war, as I think, and that
     of a kind
The viler, as underhand, not openly bearing the
     sword.

8.

Sooner or later I too may passively take the print
Of the golden age — why not? I have neither hope
     nor trust;
May make my heart as a millstone, set my face as a
     flint,
Cheat and be cheated, and die: who knows? we are
     ashes and dust.

9.

Peace sitting under her olive, and slurring the days
     gone by,
When the poor are hovell'd and hustled together,
     each sex, like swine,

When only the ledger lives, and when only not all
    men lie;
Peace in her vineyard — yes! — but a company
    forges the wine.

10.

And the vitriol madness flushes up in the ruffian's
    head,
Till the filthy by-lane rings to the yell of the
    trampled wife,
While chalk and alum and plaster are sold to the
    poor for bread,
And the spirit of murder works in the very means
    of life.

11.

And Sleep must lie down arm'd, for the villanous
    centre-bits
Grind on the wakeful ear in the hush of the moon-
    less nights,
While another is cheating the sick of a few last
    gasps, as he sits
To pestle a poison'd poison behind his crimson
    lights.

12.

When a Mammonite mother kills her babe for a
    burial fee,
And Timour-Mammon grins on a pile of children's
    bones,

Is it peace or war? better, war! loud war by land
    and by sea,
War with a thousand battles, and shaking a hundred
    thrones.

13.

For I trust if an enemy's fleet came yonder round
    by the hill,
And the rushing battle-bolt sang from the three-
    decker out of the foam,
That the smooth-faced snub-nosed rogue would leap
    from his counter and till,
And strike, if he could, were it but with his cheating
    yardwand, home. —

14.

What! am I raging alone as my father raged in his
    mood?
Must *I* too creep to the hollow and dash myself
    down and die
Rather than hold by the law that I made, never-
    more to brood
On a horror of shatter'd limbs and a wretched
    swindler's lie?

15.

Would there be sorrow for *me*? there was *love* in
    the passionate shriek,
Love for the silent thing that had made false haste
    to the grave —

Wrapt in a cloak, as I saw him, and thought he
would rise and speak
And rave at the lie and the liar, ah God, as he used
to rave.

16.

am sick of the Hall and the hill, I am sick of the
moor and the main.
Why should I stay? can a sweeter chance ever come
to me here?
O, having the nerves of motion as well as the nerves
of pain,
Were it not wise if I fled from the place and the pit
and the fear?

17.

There are workmen up at the Hall: they are coming
back from abroad;
The dark old place will be gilt by the touch of a
millionaire:
I have heard, I know not whence, of the singular
beauty of Maud;
I play'd with the girl when a child; she promised
then to be fair.

18.

Maud with her venturous climbings and tumbles and
childish escapes,
Maud the delight of the village, the ringing joy of
the Hall,

Maud with her sweet purse-mouth when my father
　　　　dangled the grapes,
Maud the beloved of my mother, the moon-faced
　　　　darling of all, —

19.

What is she now? My dreams are bad. She may
　　　　bring me a curse.
No, there is fatter game on the moor; she will let
　　　　me alone.
Thanks, for the fiend best knows whether woman
　　　　or man be the worse.
I will bury myself in my books, and the Devil may
　　　　pipe to his own.

II.

LONG have I sigh'd for a calm: God grant I may
　　　　find it at last!
It will never be broken by Maud, she has neither
　　　　savor nor salt,
But a cold and clear-cut face, as I found when her
　　　　carriage past,
Perfectly beautiful: let it be granted her: where is
　　　　the fault?
All that I saw (for her eyes were downcast, not to
　　　　be seen)
Faultily faultless, icily regular, splendidly null,
Dead perfection, no more; nothing more, if it had
　　　　not been

For a chance of travel, a paleness, an hour's defect
of the rose,
Or an underlip, you may call it a little too ripe, too
full,
Or the least delicate aquiline curve in a sensitive
nose,
From which I escaped heart-free, with the least
little touch of spleen.

III.

COLD and clear-cut face, why come you so cruelly
meek,
Breaking a slumber in which all spleenful folly was
drown'd,
Pale with the golden beam of an eyelash dead on
the cheek,
Passionless, pale, cold face, star-sweet on a gloom
profound ;
Womanlike, taking revenge too deep for a transient
wrong
Done but in thought to your beauty, and ever as
pale as before
Growing and fading and growing upon me without
a sound,
Luminous, gemlike, ghostlike, deathlike, half the
night long
Growing and fading and growing, till I could bear
it no more,
But arose, and all by myself in my own dark garden
ground,

Listening now to the tide in its broad-flung ship-
      wrecking roar,
Now to the scream of a madden'd beach dragg'd
      down by the wave,
Walk'd in a wintry wind by a ghastly glimmer, and
      found
The shining daffodil dead, and Orion low in his
      grave.

IV.

1.

A MILLION emeralds break from the ruby-budded
      lime
In the little grove where I sit — ah, wherefore can-
      not I be
Like things of the season gay, like the bountiful
      season bland,
When the far-off sail is blown by the breeze of a
      softer clime,
Half-lost in the liquid azure bloom of a crescent of
      sea,
The silent sapphire-spangled marriage ring of the
      land?

2.

Below me, there, is the village, and looks how quiet
      and small!
And yet bubbles o'er like a city, with gossip, scan-
      dal, and spite;

And Jack on his alehouse bench has as many lies as
    a Czar;
And here on the landward side, by a red rock, glim-
    mers the Hall;
And up in the high Hall-garden I see her pass like
    a light;
But sorrow seize me if ever that light be my leading
    star!

3.

When have I bow'd to her father the wrinkled head
    of the race?
I met her to-day with her brother but not to her
    brother I bow'd;
I bow'd to his lady-sister as she rode by on the
    moor;
But the fire of a foolish pride flash'd over her beau-
    tiful face.
O child, you wrong your beauty, believe it, in being
    so proud;
Your father has wealth well-gotten, and I am name-
    less and poor.

4.

I keep but a man and a maid, ever ready to slander
    and steal;
I know it, and smile a hard-set smile, like a stoic, or
    like
A wiser epicurean, and let the world have its way:
For nature is one with rapine, a harm no preacher
    can heal;

The Mayfly is torn by the swallow, the sparrow
    spear'd by the shrike,
And the whole little wood where I sit is a world of
    plunder and prey.

5.

We are puppets, Man in his pride, and Beauty fair
    in her flower,
Do we move ourselves, or are moved by an unseen
    hand at a game
That pushes us off from the board, and others ever
    succeed?
Ah yet, we cannot be kind to each other here for
    an hour;
We whisper, and hint, and chuckle, and grin at a
    brother's shame;
However we brave it out, we men are a little breed.

6.

A monstrous eft was of old the Lord and Master of
    Earth,
For him did his high sun flame, and his river billow-
    ing ran,
And he felt himself in his force to be Nature's
    crowning race.
As nine months go to the shaping an infant ripe for
    his birth,
So many a million of ages have gone to the making
    of man:
He now is first, but is he the last? is he not too
    base?

7.

The man of science himself is fonder of glory, and
    vain,
An eye well-practised in nature, a spirit bounded
    and poor;
The passionate heart of the poet is whirl'd into folly
    and vice.
I would not marvel at either, but keep a temperate
    brain;
For not to desire or admire, if a man could learn it,
    were more
Than to walk all day like the sultan of old in a gar-
    den of spice.

8.

For the drift of the Maker is dark, an Isis hid by
    the veil.
Who knows the ways of the world, how God will
    bring them about?
Our planet is one, the suns are many, the world is
    wide.
Shall I weep if a Poland fall? shall I shriek if a
    Hungary fail?
Or an infant civilization be ruled with rod or with
    knout?
I have not made the world, and He that made it
    will guide.

9.

Be mine a philosopher's life in the quiet woodland
    ways,

Where if I cannot be gay let a passionless peace be
	my lot,
Far-off from the clamor of liars belied in the hubbub
	of lies ;
From the long-neck'd geese of the world that are
	ever hissing dispraise,
Because their natures are little, and, whether he
	heed it or not,
Where each man walks with his head in a cloud of
	poisonous flies.

10.

And most of all would I flee from the cruel madness
	of love,
The honey of poison-flowers and all the measureless
	ill.
Ah Maud, you milkwhite fawn, you are all unmeet
	for a wife.
Your mother is mute in her grave as her image in
	marble above ;
Your father is ever in London, you wander about at
	your will ;
You have but fed on the roses, and lain in the lilies
	of life.

V.

1.

A VOICE by the cedar-tree,
In the meadow under the Hall !
She is singing an air that is known to me,

A passionate ballad gallant and gay,
A martial song like a trumpet's call!
Singing alone in the morning of life,
In the happy morning of life and of May
Singing of men that in battle array,
Ready in heart and ready in hand,
March with banner and bugle and fife
To the death, for their native land.

2.

Maud with her exquisite face,
And wild voice pealing up to the sunny sky,
And feet like sunny gems on an English green,
Maud in the light of her youth and her grace,
Singing of Death, and of Honor that cannot die,
Till I well could weep for a time so sordid and mean,
And myself so languid and base.

3.

Silence, beautiful voice!
Be still, for you only trouble the mind
With a joy in which I cannot rejoice,
A glory I shall not find.
Still! I will hear you no more,
For your sweetness hardly leaves me a choice
But to move to the meadow and fall before
Her feet on the meadow grass, and adore,
Not her, who is neither courtly nor kind,
Not her, not her, but a voice.

VI.

1.

MORNING arises stormy and pale,
No sun, but a wannish glare
In fold upon fold of hueless cloud,
And the budded peaks of the wood are bow'd
Caught and cuff'd by the gale:
I had fancied it would be fair.

2.

Whom but Maud should I meet
Last night, when the sunset burn'd
On the blossom'd gable-ends
At the head of the village street,
Whom but Maud should I meet?
And she touch'd my hand with a smile so sweet
She made me divine amends
For a courtesy not return'd.

3.

And thus a delicate spark
Of glowing and growing light
Thro' the livelong hours of the dark
Kept itself warm in the heart of my dreams,
Ready to burst in a color'd flame;
Till at last, when the morning came
In a cloud, it faded, and seems
But an ashen-gray delight.

4.

What if with her sunny hair,
And smile as sunny as cold,
She meant to weave me a snare
Of some coquettish deceit,
Cleopatra-like as of old
To entangle me when we met,
To have her lion roll in a silken net,
And fawn at a victor's feet.

5.

Ah, what shall I be at fifty
Should Nature keep me alive,
If I find the world so bitter
When I am but twenty-five?
Yet, if she were not a cheat,
If Maud were all that she seem'd,
And her smile were all that I dream'd,
Then the world were not so bitter
But a smile could make it sweet.

6.

What if tho' her eye seem'd full
Of a kind intent to me,
What if that dandy despot, he,
That jewell'd mass of millinery,
That oil'd and curl'd Assyrian Bull
Smelling of musk and of insolence,
Her brother, from whom I keep aloof,
Who wants the finer politic sense

To mask, tho' but in his own behoof,
With a glassy smile his brutal scorn,—
What if he had told her yestermorn
How prettily for his own sweet sake
A face of tenderness might be feign'd,
And a moist mirage in desert eyes,
That so, when the rotten hustings shake
In another month to his brazen lies,
A wretched vote may be gain'd.

7.

For a raven ever croaks, at my side,
Keep watch and ward, keep watch and ward,
Or thou wilt prove their tool.
Yea too, myself from myself I guard,
For often a man's own angry pride
Is cap and bells for a fool.

8.

Perhaps the smile and tender tone
Came out of her pitying womanhood,
For am I not, am I not, here alone
So many a summer since she died,
My mother, who was so gentle and good?
Living alone in an empty house,
Here half-hid in the gleaming wood,
Where I hear the dead at midday moan,
And the shrieking rush of the wainscot mouse,
And my own sad name in corners cried,
When the shiver of dancing leaves is thrown

About its echoing chambers wide,
Till a morbid hate and horror have grown
Of a world in which I have hardly mixt,
And a morbid eating lichen fixt
On a heart half-turn'd to stone.

9.

O heart of stone, are you flesh, and caught
By that you swore to withstand?
For what was it else within me wrought
But, I fear, the new strong wine of love,
That made my tongue so stammer and trip
When I saw the treasured splendor, her hand,
Come sliding out of her sacred glove,
And the sunlight broke from her lip?

10.

I have play'd with her when a child;
She remembers it now we meet.
Ah well, well, well, I may be beguiled
By some coquettish deceit.
Yet, if she were not a cheat,
If Maud were all that she seem'd,
And her smile had all that I dream'd,
Then the world were not so bitter
But a smile could make it sweet.

VII.

1.

Did I hear it half in a doze
  Long since, I know not where?
Did I dream it an hour ago,
  When asleep in this arm-chair?

2.

Men were drinking together,
  Drinking and talking of me;
"Well, if it prove a girl, the boy
  Will have plenty: so let it be."

3.

Is it an echo of something
  Read with a boy's delight,
Viziers nodding together
  In some Arabian night?

4.

Strange, that I hear two men,
  Somewhere talking of me;
"Well, if it prove a girl, my boy
  Will have plenty: so let it be."

VIII.

She came to the village church,
  And sat by a pillar alone;

An angel watching an urn
Wept over her, carved in stone;
And once, but once, she lifted her eyes,
And suddenly, sweetly, strangely blush'd
To find they were met by my own;
And suddenly, sweetly, my heart beat stronger
And thicker, until I heard no longer
The snowy-banded, dilettante,
Delicate-handed priest intone;
And thought, is it pride, and mused and sigh'd
"No surely, now it cannot be pride."

IX.

I was walking a mile,
More than a mile from the shore,
The sun look'd out with a smile
Betwixt the cloud and the moor,
And riding at set of day
Over the dark moor land,
Rapidly riding far away,
She waved to me with her hand.
There were two at her side,
Something flash'd in the sun,
Down by the hill I saw them ride,
In a moment they were gone:
Like a sudden spark
Struck vainly in the night,
And back returns the dark
With no more hope of light.

X.

1.

Sick, am I sick of a jealous dread?
Was not one of the two at her side
This new-made lord, whose splendor plucks
The slavish hat from the villager's head?
Whose old grandfather has lately died,
Gone to a blacker pit, for whom
Grimy nakedness dragging his trucks
And laying his trams in a poison'd gloom
Wrought till he crept from a gutted mine
Master of half a servile shire,
And left his coal all turn'd into gold
To a grandson, first of his noble line,
Rich in the grace all women desire,
Strong in the power that all men adore,
And simper and set their voices lower,
And soften as if to a girl, and hold
Awe-stricken breaths at a work divine,
Seeing his gew-gaw castle shine,
New as his title, built last year,
There amid perky larches and pine,
And over the sullen-purple moor
(Look at it) pricking a cockney ear.

2.

What, has he found my jewel out?
For one of the two that rode at her side
Bound for the Hall, I am sure was he:

Bound for the Hall, and I think for a bride.
Blithe would her brother's acceptance be.
Maud could be gracious too, no doubt,
To a lord, a captain, a padded shape,
A bought commission, a waxen face,
A rabbit mouth that is ever agape —
Bought? what is it he cannot buy?
And therefore splenetic, personal, base,
A wounded thing with a rancorous cry,
At war with myself and a wretched race,
Sick, sick to the heart of life, am I.

3.

Last week came one to the county town,
To preach our poor little army down,
And play the game of the despot kings,
Tho' the state has done it and thrice as well:
This broad-brim'd hawker of holy things,
Whose ear is stuff'd with his cotton, and rings
Even in dreams to the chink of his pence,
This huckster put down war! can he tell
Whether war be a cause or a consequence?
Put down the passions that make earth Hell!
Down with ambition, avarice, pride,
Jealousy, down! cut off from the mind
The bitter springs of anger and fear;
Down too, down at your own fireside,
With the evil tongue and the evil ear,
For each is at war with mankind.

4.

I wish I could hear again
The chivalrous battle-song
That she warbled alone in her joy!
I might persuade myself then
She would not do herself this great wrong
To take a wanton, dissolute boy
For a man and leader of men.

5.

Ah God, for a man with heart, head, hand,
Like some of the simple great ones gone
Forever and ever by,
One still strong man in a blatant land,
Whatever they call him, what care I,
Aristocrat, democrat, autocrat, — one
Who can rule and dare not lie.

6.

And ah for a man to rise in me,
That the man I am may cease to be!

XI.

1.

O LET the solid ground
    Not fail beneath my feet
Before my life has found
    What some have found so sweet ;

Then let come what come **may**,
What matter if I go mad,
I shall have had my day.

2.

Let the sweet heavens endure,
    Not close and darken above **me**
Before I am quite quite sure
    That there is one to love me;
Then let come what come may
To a life that has been so sad,
I shall have had my day.

XII.

1.

Birds in the high Hall-garden
    When twilight was falling,
Maud, Maud, Maud, Maud,
    They were crying and calling.

2.

Where was Maud? in our wood;
    And I, who else, was with her,
Gathering woodland lilies,
    Myriads blow together.

3.

Birds in our woods sang
    Ringing thro' the valleys,
Maud is here, here, here
    In among the lilies.

4.

I kiss'd her slender hand,
   She took the kiss sedately;
Maud is not seventeen,
   But she is tall and stately.

5.

I to cry out on pride
   Who have won her favor!
O Maud were sure of Heaven
   If lowliness could save her.

6.

I know the way she went
   Home with her maiden posy,
For her feet have touch'd the meadows
   And left the daisies rosy.

7.

Birds in the high Hall-garden
   Were crying and calling to her,
Where is Maud, Maud, Maud,
   One is come to woo her.

8.

Look, a horse at the door,
   And little King Charles is snarling,
Go back, my lord, across the moor,
   You are not her darling.

XIII.

1.

Scorn'd, to be scorn'd by one that I scorn,
Is that a matter to make me fret?
That a calamity hard to be borne?
Well, he may live to hate me yet.
Fool that I am to be vext with his pride!
I past him, I was crossing his lands;
He stood on the path a little aside;
His face, as I grant, in spite of spite,
Has a broad-blown comeliness, red and white,
And six feet two, as I think, he stands;
But his essence turn'd the live air sick,
And barbarous opulence jewel-thick
Sunn'd itself on his breast and his hands.

2.

Who shall call me ungentle, unfair,
I long'd so heartily then and there
To give him the grasp of fellowship;
But while I past he was humming an air,
Stopt, and then with a riding whip
Leisurely tapping a glossy boot,
And curving a contumelious lip,
Gorgonized me from head to foot
With a stony British stare.

3.

Why sits he here in his father's chair?
That old man never comes to his place:
Shall I believe him ashamed to be seen?
For only once, in the village street,
Last year, I caught a glimpse of his face,
A gray old wolf and a lean.
Scarcely, now, would I call him a cheat;
For then, perhaps, as a child of deceit,
She might by a true descent be untrue;
And Maud is as true as Maud is sweet;
Tho' I fancy her sweetness only due
To the sweeter blood by the other side;
Her mother has been a thing complete,
However she came to be so allied.
And fair without, faithful within,
Maud to him is nothing akin;
Some peculiar mystic grace
Made her only the child of her mother,
And heap'd the whole inherited sin
On that huge scapegoat of the race,
All, all upon the brother.

4.

Peace, angry spirit, and let him be!
Has not his sister smiled on me?

XIV.

1.

MAUD has a garden of roses
And lilies fair on a lawn;

There she walks in her state
And tends upon bed and bower
And thither I climb'd at dawn
And stood by her garden gate;
A lion ramps at the top,
He is claspt by a passion flower.

2.

Maud's own little oak-room
(Which Maud, like a precious stone
Set in the heart of the carven gloom,
Lights with herself, when alone
She sits by her music and books,
And her brother lingers late
With a roistering company) looks
Upon Maud's own garden gate:
And I thought as I stood, if a hand, as white
As ocean-foam in the moon, were laid
On the hasp of the window, and my Delight
Had a sudden desire, like a glorious ghost, to glide,
Like a beam of the seventh Heaven, down to my
    side,
There were but a step to be made.

3.

The fancy flatter'd my mind,
And again seem'd overbold;
Now I thought that she cared for me,
Now I thought she was kind
Only because she was cold.

4.

I heard no sound where I stood
But the rivulet on from the lawn
Running down to my own dark wood
Or the voice of the long sea-wave as it swell'd
Now and then in the dim-gray dawn;
But I look'd, and round, all round the house I beheld
The death-white curtain drawn;
Felt a horror over me creep,
Prickle my skin and catch my breath,
Knew that the death-white curtain meant but sleep,
Yet I shudder'd and thought like a fool of the sleep
    of death.

XV.

So dark a mind within me dwells,
    And I make myself such evil cheer,
That if I be dear to some one else,
    Then some one else may have much to fear;
But if I be dear to some one else,
    Then I should be to myself more dear.
Shall I not take care of all that I think,
Yea ev'n of wretched meat and drink,
If I be dear,
If I be dear to some one else?

XVI.

I.

THIS lump of earth has left his estate
The lighter by the loss of his weight;

And so that he find what he went to seek,
And fulsome Pleasure clog him, and drown
His heart in the gross mud-honey of town,
He may stay for a year who has gone for a week;
But this is the day when I must speak,
And I see my Oread coming down,
O this is the day!
O beautiful creature, what am I
That I dare to look her way;
Think I may hold dominion sweet,
Lord of the pulse that is lord of her breast,
And dream of her beauty with tender dread,
From the delicate Arab arch of her feet
To the grace that, bright and light as the crest
Of a peacock, sits on her shining head,
And she knows it not: O, if she knew it,
To know her beauty might half undo it.
I know it the one bright thing to save
My yet young life in the wilds of Time,
Perhaps from madness, perhaps from crime,
Perhaps from a selfish grave.

2.

What, if she were fasten'd to this fool lord,
Dare I bid her abide by her word?
Should I love her so well if she
Had given her word to a thing so low?
Shall I love her as well as if she
Can break her word were it even for me?
I trust that it is not so.

3.

Catch not my breath, O clamorous heart,
Let not my tongue be a thrall to my eye,
For I must tell her before we part,
I must tell her, or die.

XVII.

Go not, happy day,
    From the shining fields,
Go not, happy day,
    Till the maiden yields.
Rosy is the West,
    Rosy is the South,
Roses are her cheeks,
    And a rose her mouth.
When the happy Yes
    Falters from her lips,
Pass and blush the news
    O'er the blowing ships,
Over blowing seas,
    Over seas at rest,
Pass the happy news,
    Blush it thro' the West,
Till the red man dance
    By his red cedar-tree,
And the red man's babe
    Leap, beyond the sea.
Blush from West to East,
    Blush from East to West,

Till the West is East,
    Blush it thro' the West.
Rosy is the West,
    Rosy is the South,
Roses are her cheeks,
    And a rose her mouth.

XVIII.

1.

I HAVE led her home, my love, my only friend.
There is none like her, none,
And never yet so warmly ran my blood
And sweetly, on and on
Calming itself to the long-wish'd for end,
Full to the banks, close on the promised good.

2.

None like her, none
Just now the dry-tongued laurel's pattering talk
Seem'd her light foot along the garden walk,
And shook my heart to think she comes once more;
But even then I heard her close the door,
The gates of Heaven are closed, and she is gone.

3.

There is none like her, none.
Nor will be when our summers have deceased.
O, art thou sighing for Lebanon
In the long breeze that streams to thy delicious East,

Sighing for Lebanon,
Dark cedar, tho' thy limbs have here increased,
Upon a pastoral slope as fair,
And looking to the South, and fed
With honey'd rain and delicate air,
And haunted by the starry head
Of her whose gentle will has changed my fate,
And made my life a perfumed altar-flame;
And over whom thy darkness must have spread
With such delight as theirs of old, thy great
Forefathers of the thornless garden, there
Shadowing the snow-limb'd Eve from whom she
        came.

4.

Here will I lie, while these long branches sway,
And you fair stars that crown a happy day
Go in and out as if at merry play,
Who am no more so all forlorn,
As when it seem'd far better to be born
To labor and the mattock-harden'd hand,
Than nursed its ease and brought to understand
A sad astrology, the boundless plan
That makes you tyrants in your iron skies,
Innumerable, pitiless, passionless eyes,
Cold fires, yet with power to burn and brand
His nothingness into man.

5.

But now shine on, and what care I,
Who in this stormy gulf have found a pearl

The countercharm of space and hollow sky,
And do accept my madness and would die
To save from some slight shame one simple girl.

6.

Would die; for sullen seeming Death may give
More life to Love than is or ever was
In our low world, where yet 'tis sweet to live,
Let no one ask me how it came to pass;
It seems that I am happy, that to me
A livelier emerald twinkles in the grass,
A purer sapphire melts into the sea.

7.

Not die; but live a life of truest breath,
And teach true life to fight with mortal wrongs.
O, why should Love, like men in drinking-songs,
Spice his fair banquet with the dust of death?
Make answer, Maud my bliss.
Maud made my Maud by that long lover's kiss,
Life of my life, wilt thou not answer this?
"The dusky strand of Death inwoven here
With dear Love's tie, makes Love himself more
    dear."

8.

Is that enchanted moan only the swell
Of the long waves that roll in yonder bay?
And hark the clock within, the silver knell
Of twelve sweet hours that past in bridal white,
And died to live, long as my pulses play;

But now by this my love has closed her sight
And given false death her hand, and stol'n away
To dreamful wastes where footless fancies dwell
Among the fragments of the golden day.
May nothing there her maiden grace affright;
Dear heart, I feel with thee the drowsy spell.
My bride to be, my evermore delight,
My own heart's heart and ownest own farewell;
It is but for a little space I go
And ye meanwhile far over moor and fell
Beat to the noiseless music of the night!
Has our whole earth gone nearer to the glow
Of your soft splendors that you look so bright?
I have climb'd nearer out of lonely Hell.
Beat, happy stars, timing with things below,
Beat with my heart more blest than heart can tell,
Blest, but for some dark undercurrent woe
That seems to draw — but it shall not be so:
Let all be well, be well.

XIX.

1.

HER brother is coming back to-night,
Breaking up my dream of delight.

2.

My dream? do I dream of bliss?
I have walk'd awake with Truth.

O when did a morning shine
So rich in atonement as this
For my dark-dawning youth,
Darken'd watching a mother decline
And that dead man at her heart and mine:
For who was left to watch her but I?
Yet so did I let my freshness die.

3.

I trust that I did not talk
To gentle Maud in our walk
(For often in lonely wanderings
I have cursed him even to lifeless things)
But I trust that I did not talk,
Not touch on her father's sin:
I am sure I did but speak
Of my mother's faded cheek
When it slowly grew so thin,
That I felt she was slowly dying
Vext with lawyers and harass'd with debt:
For how often I caught her with eyes all wet,
Shaking her head at her son and sighing
A world of trouble within!

4.

And Maud too, Maud was moved
To speak of the mother she loved
As one scarce less forlorn,
Dying abroad and it seems apart
From him who had ceased to share her heart,
And ever mourning over the feud,

The household Fury sprinkled with blood
By which our houses are torn;
How strange was what she said,
When only Maud and the brother
Hung over her dying bed, —
That Maud's dark father and mine
Had bound us one to the other,
Betrothed us over their wine
On the day when Maud was born;
Seal'd her mine from her first sweet breath.
Mine, mine by a right, from birth till death,
Mine, mine — our fathers have sworn.

5.

But the true blood spilt had in it a heat
To dissolve the precious seal on a bond,
That, if left uncancell'd, had been so sweet:
And none of us thought of a something beyond,
A desire that awoke in the heart of the child,
As it were a duty done to the tomb,
To be friends for her sake, to be reconciled;
And I was cursing them and my doom,
And letting a dangerous thought run wild
While often abroad in the fragrant gloom
Of foreign churches, — I see her there,
Bright English lily, breathing a prayer
To be friends, to be reconciled!

6.

But then what a flint is he!
Abroad, at Florence, at Rome,

I find whenever she touch'd on me
This brother had laugh'd her down,
And at last, when each came home,
He had darken'd into a frown,
Chid her, and forbid her to speak
To me, her friend of the years before;
And this was what had redden'd her cheek,
When I bow'd to her on the moor.

7.

Yet Maud, altho' not blind
To the faults of his heart and mind,
I see she cannot but love him,
And says he is rough but kind,
And wishes me to approve him,
And tells me, when she lay
Sick once, with a fear of worse,
That he left his wine and horses and play,
Sat with her, read to her, night and day,
And tended her like a nurse.

8.

Kind? but the death-bed desire
Spurn'd by this heir of the liar —
Rough but kind? yet I know
He has plotted against me in this,
That he plots against me still.
Kind to Maud? that were not amiss,
Well, rough but kind; why, let it be so:
For shall not Maud have her will?

9.

For, Maud, so tender and true,
As long as my life endures
I feel I shall owe you a debt,
That I never can hope to pay;
And if ever I should forget
That I owe this debt to you
And for your sweet sake to yours;
O then, what then shall I say?—
If ever I *should* forget,
May God make me more wretched
Than ever I have been yet!

10.

So now I have sworn to bury
All this dead body of hate,
I feel so free and so clear
By the loss of that dead weight,
That I should grow light-headed, I fear,
Fantastically merry;
But that her brother comes, like a blight
On my fresh hope, to the Hall to-night.

XX.

1.

Strange, that I felt so gay,
Strange, that I tried to-day
To beguile her melancholy;
The Sultan, as we name him,
She did not wish to blame him—

But he vext her and perplext her
With his worldly talk and folly:
Was it gentle to reprove her
For stealing out of view
From a little lazy lover
Who but claims her as his due?
Or for chilling his caresses,
By the coldness of her manners,
Nay, the plainness of her dresses?
Now I know her but in two,
Nor can pronounce upon it
If one should ask me whether
The habit, hat, and feather,
Or the frock and gypsy bonnet
Be the neater and completer;
For nothing can be sweeter
Than maiden Maud in either.

2.

But to-morrow, if we live,
Our ponderous squire will give
A grand political dinner
To half the squirelings near;
And Maud will wear her jewels,
And the bird of prey will hover,
And the titmouse hope to win her
With his chirrup at her ear.

3.

A grand political dinner
To the men of many acres,

A gathering of the Tory,
A dinner and then a dance
For the maids and marriage-makers,
And every eye but mine will glance
At Maud in all her glory.

4.

For I am not invited,
But, with the Sultan's pardon,
I am all as well delighted,
For I know her own rose-garden,
And mean to linger in it
Till the dancing will be over;
And then, O then, come out to me
For a minute, but for a minute,
Come out to your own true lover,
That your true lover may see
Your glory also, and render
All homage to his own darling,
Queen Maud in all her splendor.

XXI.

RIVULET crossing my ground,
And bringing me down from the Hall
This garden-rose that I found,
Forgetful of Maud and me,
And lost in trouble and moving round
Here at the head of a tinkling fall,
And trying to pass to the sea;
O Rivulet, born at the Hall,

My Maud has sent it by thee
(If I read her sweet will right)
On a blushing mission to me,
Saying in odor and color, " Ah, be
Among the roses to-night."

XXII.

1.

COME into the garden, Maud,
For the black bat, night, has flown,
Come into the garden, Maud,
I am here at the gate alone ;
And the woodbine spices are wafted abroad,
And the musk of the roses blown.

2.

For a breeze of morning moves,
And the planet of Love is on high,
Beginning to faint in the light that she loves
On a bed of daffodil sky,
To faint in the light of the sun she loves,
To faint in his light, and to die.

3.

All night have the roses heard
The flute, violin, bassoon ;
All night has the casement jessamine stirr'd
To the dancers dancing in tune ;
Till a silence fell with the waking bird,
And a hush with the setting moon.

4.

I said to the lily, " There is but one
   With whom she has heart to be gay.
When will the dancers leave her alone?
   She is weary of dance and play."
Now half to the setting moon are gone,
   And half to the rising day;
Low on the sand and loud on the stone
   The last wheel echoes away.

5.

I said to the rose, " The brief night goes
   In babble and revel and wine.
O young lord-lover, what sighs are those,
   For one that will never be thine?
But mine, but mine," so I sware to the rose,
   "Forever and ever, mine."

6.

And the soul of the rose went into my blood,
   As the music clash'd in the hall;
As long by the garden lake I stood,
   For I heard your rivulet fall
From the lake to the meadow and on to the wood,
   Our wood, that is dearer than all;

7.

From the meadow your walks have left so sweet
   That whenever a March-wind sighs
He sets the jewel-print of your feet
   In violets blue as your eyes,

To the woody hollows in which we meet
    And the valleys of Paradise.

8.

The slender acacia would not shake
    One long milk-bloom on the tree;
The white lake-blossom fell into the lake,
    As the pimpernel dozed on the lea;
But the rose was awake all night for your sake,
    Knowing your promise to me;
The lilies and roses were all awake,
    They sigh'd for the dawn and thee.

9.

Queen rose of the rosebud garden of girls,
    Come hither, the dances are done,
In gloss of satin and glimmer of pearls,
    Queen lily and rose in one;
Shine out, little head, sunning over with curls,
    To the flowers, and be their sun.

10.

There has fallen a splendid tear
    From the passion-flower at the gate.
She is coming, my dove, my dear;
    She is coming, my life, my fate;
The red rose cries, "She is near, she is near;"
    And the white rose weeps, "She is late;"
The larkspur listens, "I hear, I hear;"
    And the lily whispers, "I wait."

II.

She is coming, my own, my sweet;
    Were it ever so airy a tread,
My heart would hear her and beat,
    Were it earth in an earthy bed;
My dust would hear her and beat,
    Had I lain for a century dead;
Would start and tremble under her feet,
    And blossom in purple and red.

XXIII.

I.

"THE fault was mine, the fault was mine"—
Why am I sitting here so stunn'd and still,
Plucking the harmless wild-flower on the hill?—
It is this guilty hand!—
And there rises ever a passionate cry
From underneath in the darkening land—
What is it, that has been done?
O dawn of Eden bright over earth and sky,
The fires of Hell brake out of thy rising sun,
The fires of Hell and of Hate;
For she, sweet soul, had hardly spoken a word,
When her brother ran in his rage to the gate,
He came with the babe-faced lord;
Heap'd on her terms of disgrace,
And while she wept, and I strove to be cool,
He fiercely gave me the lie,
Till I with as fierce an anger spoke,

And he struck me, madman, over the face,
Struck me before the languid fool,
Who was gaping and grinning by:
Struck for himself an evil stroke:
Wrought for his house an irredeemable woe;
For front to front in an hour we stood,
And a million horrible bellowing echoes broke
From the red-ribb'd hollow behind the wood,
And thunder'd up into Heaven the Christless code,
That must have life for a blow.
Ever and ever afresh they seem'd to grow.
Was it he lay there with a fading eye?
"The fault was mine," he whisper'd, "fly!"
Then glided out of the joyous wood
The ghastly Wraith of one that I know; .
And there rang on a sudden a passionate cry,
A cry for a brother's blood:
It will ring in my heart and my ears, till I die, till I
    die.

2.

Is it gone? my pulses beat—
What was it? a lying trick of the brain?
Yet I thought I saw her stand,
A shadow there at my feet,
High over the shadowy land.
It is gone; and the heavens fall in a gentle rain,
When they should burst and drown with deluging
    storms
The feeble vassals of wine and anger and lust,
The little hearts that know not how to forgive:

Arise, my God, and strike, for we hold Thee just,
Strike dead the whole weak race of venomous worms,
That sting each other here in the dust;
We are not worthy to live.

XXIV.

I.

SEE what a lovely shell,
Small and pure as a pearl,
Lying close to my foot,
Frail, but a work divine,
Made so fairly well
With delicate spire and whorl,
How exquisitely minute,
A miracle of design!

2.

What is it? a learned man
Could give it a clumsy name.
Let him name it who can,
The beauty would be the same.

3.

The tiny cell is forlorn,
Void of the little living will
That made it stir on the shore.
Did he stand at the diamond door
Of his house in a rainbow frill?
Did he push, when he was uncurl'd,
A golden foot or a fairy horn
Thro' his dim water-world?

4.

Slight, to be crush'd with a tap
Of my finger-nail on the sand,
Small, but a work divine,
Frail, but of force to withstand,
Year upon year, the shock
Of cataract seas that snap
The three-decker's oaken spine
Athwart the ledges of rock,
Here on the Breton strand!

5.

Breton, not Briton; here
Like a shipwreck'd man on a coast
Of ancient fable and fear, —
Plagued with a flitting to and fro,
A disease, a hard mechanic ghost
That never came from on high
Nor never arose from below,
But only moves with the moving eye,
Flying along the land and the main, —
Why should it look like Maud?
Am I to be overawed
By what I cannot but know
Is a juggle born of the brain?

6.

Back from the Breton coast,
Sick of a nameless fear,

Back to the dark sea-line
Looking, thinking of all I have lost;
An old song vexes my ear;
But that of Lamech is mine.

7.

For years, a measureless ill,
For years, forever, to part, —
But she, she would love me still;
And as long, O God, as she
Have a grain of love for me,
So long, no doubt, no doubt,
Shall I nurse in my dark heart,
However weary, a spark of will
Not to be trampled out.

8.

Strange, that the mind, when fraught
With a passion so intense
One would think that it well
Might drown all life in the eye, —
That it should, by being so overwrought,
Suddenly strike on a sharper sense
For a shell, or a flower, little things
Which else would have been past by'
And now I remember, I,
When he lay dying there,
I noticed one of his many rings
(For he had many, poor worm) and thought
It is his mother's hair.

9.

Who knows if he be dead?
Whether I need have fled?
Am I guilty of blood?
However this may be,
Comfort her, comfort her, all things good,
While I am over the sea!
Let me and my passionate love go by,
But speak to her all things holy and high,
Whatever happen to me!
Me and my harmful love go by;
But come to her waking, find her asleep,
Powers of the height, powers of the deep,
And comfort her tho' I die.

XXV.

COURAGE, poor heart of stone!
I will not ask thee why
Thou canst not understand
That thou art left forever alone:
Courage, poor stupid heart of stone. —
Or if I ask thee why,
Care not thou to reply:
She is but dead, and the time is at hand
When thou shalt more than die.

XXVI.

I.

O THAT 'twere possible
After long grief and pain

To find the arms of my true love
Round me once again!

2.

When I was wont to meet her
In the silent woody places
By the home that gave me birth,
We stood tranced in long embraces
Mixt with kisses sweeter sweeter
Than any thing on earth.

3.

A shadow flits before me,
Not thou, but like to thee;
Ah Christ, that it were possible
For one short hour to see
The souls we loved, that they might tell us
What and where they be.

4.

It leads me forth at evening,
It lightly winds and steals
In a cold white robe before me,
When all my spirit reels
At the shouts, the leagues of lights,
And the roaring of the wheels.

5.

Half the night I waste in sighs,
Half in dreams I sorrow after

The delight of early skies;
In a wakeful dose I sorrow
For the hand, the lips, the eyes,
For the meeting of the morrow,
The delight of happy laughter,
The delight of low replies.

6.

Tis a morning pure and sweet,
And a dewy splendor falls
On the little flower that clings
To the turrets and the walls;
'Tis a morning pure and sweet,
And the light and shadow fleet;
She is walking in the meadow,
And the woodland echo rings;
In a moment we shall meet;
She is singing in the meadow,
And the rivulet at her feet
Ripples on in light and shadow
To the ballad that she sings.

7.

Do I hear her sing as of old,
My bird with the shining head,
My own dove with the tender eye?
But there rings on a sudden a passionate **cry**,
There is some one dying or dead,
And a sullen thunder is roll'd;
For a tumult shakes the city,

And I wake, my dream is fled;
In the shuddering dawn, behold,
Without knowledge, without pit**y**,
By the curtains of my bed
That abiding phantom cold.

8.

Get thee thence, nor come again,
Mix not memory with doubt,
Pass, thou deathlike type of pain,
Pass and cease to move about,
'Tis the blot upon the brain
That *will* show itself without.

9.

Then I rise, the eavedrops fall,
And the yellow vapors choke
The great city sounding wide;
The day comes, a dull red ball
Wrapt in drifts of lurid smoke
On the misty river-tide.

10.

Thro' the hubbub of the market
I steal, a wasted frame,
It crosses here, it crosses there,
Thro' all that crowd confused and loud
The shadow still the same;
And on thy heavy eyelids
My anguish hangs like shame.

II.

Alas for her that met me,
That heard me softly call,
Came glimmering thro' the laurels
At the quiet evenfall,
In the garden by the turrets
Of the old manorial hall.

12.

Would the happy spirit descend,
From the realms of light and song,
In the chamber or the street,
As she looks among the blest,
Should I fear to greet my friend
Or to say "forgive the wrong,"
Or to ask her, "take me sweet,
To the regions of thy rest?"

13.

But the broad light glares and beats,
And the shadow flits and fleets
And will not let me be;
And I loathe the squares and streets,
And the faces that one meets,
Hearts with no love for me:
Always I long to creep
Into some still cavern deep,
There to weep, and weep, and weep
My whole soul out to thee.

XXVII.

1.

Dead, long dead,
Long dead!
And my heart is a handful of dust,
And the wheels go over my head,
And my bones are shaken with pain,
For into a shallow grave they are thrust,
Only a yard beneath the street,
And the hoofs of the horses beat, beat,
The hoofs of the horses beat,
Beat into my scalp and my brain,
With never an end to the stream of passing feet,
Driving, hurrying, marrying, burying,
Clamor and rumble, and ringing and clatter,
And here beneath it is all as bad,
For I thought the dead had peace, but it is not so;
To have no peace in the grave, is that not sad?
But up and down and to and fro,
Ever about me the dead men go;
And then to hear a dead man chatter
Is enough to drive one mad.

2.

Wretchedest age, since Time began,
They cannot even bury a man;
And tho' we paid our tithes in the days that are gone,
Not a bell was rung, not a prayer was read;
It is that which makes us loud in the world of the
    dead;

There is none that does his work, not one:
A touch of their office might have sufficed,
But the churchmen fain would kill their church,
As the churches have kill'd their Christ.

3.

See, there is one of us sobbing,
No limit to his distress;
And another, a lord of all things, praying
To his own great self, as I guess;
And another, a statesman there, betraying
His party-secret, fool, to the press;
And yonder a vile physician, babbling
The case of his patient, — all for what?
To tickle the maggot born in an empty head,
And wheedle a world that loves him not,
For it is but a world of the dead.

4.

Nothing but idiot gabble!
For the prophecy given of old
And then not understood,
Has come to pass as foretold;
Not let any man think for the public good,
But babble, merely for babble.
For I never whisper'd a private affair
Within the hearing of cat or mouse,
No, not to myself in the closet alone,
But I heard it shouted at once from the top of the
    house;

Everything came to be known:
Who told *him* we were there?

5.

Not that gray old wolf, for he came not back
From the wilderness, full of wolves, where he used
     to lie;
He has gather'd the bones for his o'ergrown whelp
     to crack;
Crack them now for yourself, and howl, and die.

6.

Prophet, curse me the babbling lip,
And curse me the British vermin, the rat;
I know not whether he came in the Hanover ship,
But I know that he lies and listens mute
In an ancient mansion's crannies and holes:
Arsenic, arsenic, sure, would do it,
Except that now we poison our babes, poor souls!
It is all used up for that.

7.

Tell him now: she is standing here at my head;
Not beautiful now, not even kind;
He may take her now; for she never speaks her
     mind,
But is ever the one thing silent here.
She is not of us, as I divine;
She comes from another stiller world of the dead,
Stiller, not fairer than mine.

8.

But I know where a garden grows,
Fairer than aught in the world beside,
All made up of the lily and rose
That blow by night, when the season is good,
To the sound of dancing music and flutes:
It is only flowers, they had no fruits,
And I almost fear they are not roses, but blood;
For the keeper was one, so full of pride,
He linkt a dead man there to a spectral bride;
For he, if he had not been a Sultan of brutes,
Would he have that hole in his side?

9.

But what will the old man say?
He laid a cruel snare in a pit
To catch a friend of mine one stormy day;
Yet now I could even weep to think of it;
For what will the old man say
When he comes to the second corpse in the pit?

10.

Friend, to be struck by the public foe,
Then to strike him and lay him low,
That were a public merit, far,
Whatever the Quaker holds, from sin;
But the red life spilt for a private blow —
I swear to you, lawful and lawless war
Are scarcely even akin.

II.

O me, why have they not buried me deep enough?
Is it kind to have made me a grave so rough,
Me, that was never a quiet sleeper?
Maybe still I am but half-dead;
Then I cannot be wholly dumb;
I will cry to the steps above my head,
And somebody, surely, some kind heart will come
To bury me, bury me
Deeper, ever so little deeper.

XXVIII.

I.

My life has crept so long on a broken wing
Thro' cells of madness, haunts of horror and fear,
That I come to be grateful at last for a little thing:
My mood is changed, for it fell at a time of year
When the face of the night is fair on the dewy
        downs,
And the shining daffodil dies, and the Charioteer
And starry Gemini hang like glorious crowns
Over Orion's grave low down in the west,
That like a silent lightning under the stars
She seem'd to divide in a dream from a band of the
        blest,
And spoke of a hope for the world in the coming
        wars —
"And in that hope, dear soul, let trouble have rest,

Knowing I tarry for thee," and pointed to Mars
As he glow'd like a ruddy shield on the Lion's
    breast.

2.

And it was but a dream, yet it yielded a dear de-
    light
To have looked, tho' but in a dream, upon eyes so
    fair,
That had been in a weary world my one thing
    bright;
And it was but a dream, yet it lighten'd my despair
When I thought that a war would arise in defence
    of the right,
That an iron tyranny now should bend or cease,
The glory of manhood stand on his ancient height,
Nor Britain's one sole God be the millionaire:
No more shall commerce be all in all, and Peace
Pipe on her pastoral hillock a languid note,
And watch her harvest ripen, her herd increase,
Nor the cannon-bullet rust on a slothful shore,
And the cobweb woven across the cannon's throat
Shall shake its threaded tears in the wind no more.

3.

And as months ran on and rumor of battle grew,
" It is time, it is time, O passionate heart," said I
(For I cleaved to a cause that I felt to be pure and
    true),
" It is time, O passionate heart and morbid eye,
That old hysterical mock-disease should die."

And I stood on a giant deck and mix'd my breath
With a loyal people shouting a battle cry,
Till I saw the dreary phantom arise and fly
Far into the North, and battle, and seas of death.

4.

Let it go or stay, so I wake to the higher aims
Of a land that has lost for a little her lust of gold,
And love of a peace that was full of wrongs and
        shames,
Horrible, hateful, monstrous, not to be told ;
And hail once more to the banner of battle
        unroll'd !
Tho' many a light shall darken, and many shall
        weep
For those that are crush'd in the clash of jarring
        claims,
Yet God's just wrath shall be wreak'd on a giant
        liar ;
And many a darkness into the light shall leap,
And shine in the sudden making of splendid
        names,
And noble thought be freer under the sun,
And the heart of a people beat with one desire ;
For the peace, that I deem'd no peace, is over and
        done,
And now by the side of the Black and the Baltic
        deep,
And deathful-grinning mouths of the fortress flames
The blood-red blossom of war with a heart of fire.

5

Let it flame or fade, and the war roll down like a
wind,

We have proved we have hearts in a cause, we are
noble still,

And myself have awaked, as it seems, to the better
mind;

It is better to fight for the good, than to rail at the
ill;

I have felt with my native land, I am one with my
kind,

I embrace the purpose of God, and the doom as-
sign'd.

THE HOLY GRAIL.

FROM noiseful arms, and acts of prowess done
In tournament or tilt, Sir Percivale,
Whom Arthur and his knighthood call'd The Pure,
Had pass'd into the silent life of prayer,
Praise, fast, and alms; and leaving for the cowl
The helmet in an abbey far away
From Camelot, there, and not long after, died.

And one, a fellow-monk among the rest,
Ambrosius, loved him much beyond the rest,
And honor'd him, and wrought into his heart
A way by love that waken'd love within,
To answer that which came: and as they sat
Beneath a world-old yew-tree, darkening half
The cloisters, on a gustful April morn
That puff'd the swaying branches into smoke
Above them, ere the summer when he died,
The monk Ambrosius question'd Percivale:

"O brother, I have seen this yew-tree smoke,
Spring after spring, for half a hundred years:
For never have I known the world without,

Nor ever stray'd beyond the pale: but thee,
When first thou camest — such a courtesy
Spake thro' the limbs and in the voice — I knew
For one of those who eat in Arthur's hall;
For good ye are and bad, and like to coins,
Some true, some light, but every one of you
Stamp'd with the image of the King; and now
Tell me, what drove thee from the Table Round,
My brother? was it earthly passion crost?

"Nay," said the knight; "for no such passion mine.
But the sweet vision of the Holy Grail
Drove me from all vainglories, rivalries,
And earthly heats that spring and sparkle out
Among us in the jousts, while women watch
Who wins, who falls; and waste the spiritual strength
Within us, better offer'd up to Heaven."

To whom the monk: "The Holy Grail! — I trust
We are green in Heaven's eyes; but here too much
We moulder — as to things without I mean —
Yet one of your own knights, a guest of ours,
Told us of this in our refectory,
But spake with such a sadness and so low
We heard not half of what he said.   What is it?
The phantom of a cup that comes and goes?"

"Nay, monk! what phantom?" answer'd Percivale,
"The cup, the cup itself, from which our Lord
Drank at the last sad supper with his own.
This, from the blessed land of Aromat —

After the day of darkness, when the dead
Went wandering o'er Moriah — the good saint,
Arimathæan Joseph, journeying brought
To Glastonbury, where the winter thorn
Blossoms at Christmas, mindful of our Lord.
And there awhile it bode; and if a man
Could touch or see it, he was heal'd at once,
By faith, of all his ills. But then the times
Grew to such evil that the holy cup
Was caught away to Heaven, and disappear'd."

To whom the monk: "From our old books I know
That Joseph came of old to Glastonbury,
And there the heathen Prince, Arviragus,
Gave him an isle of marsh whereon to build;
And there he built with wattles from the marsh
A little lonely church in days of yore,
For so they say, these books of ours, but seem
Mute of this miracle, far as I have read.
But who first saw the holy thing to-day?"

"A woman," answer'd Percivale, a nun,
And one no further off in blood from me
Than sister; and if ever holy maid
With knees of adoration wore the stone,
A holy maid; tho' never maiden glow'd,
But that was in her earlier maidenhood,
With such a fervent flame of human love,
Which being rudely blunted, glanced and shot
Only to holy things; to prayer and praise
She gave herself, to fast and alms. And yet,

Nun as she was, the scandal of the Court,
Sin against Arthur and the Table Round,
And the strange sound of an adulterous race,
Across the iron grating of her cell
Beat, and she pray'd and fasted all the more.

"And he to whom she told her sins, or what
Her all but utter whiteness held for sin,
A man wellnigh a hundred winters old,
Spake often with her of the Holy Grail,
A legend handed down thro' five or six,
And each of these a hundred winters old,
From our Lord's time.   And when King Arthur made
His Table Round, and all men's hearts became
Clean for a season, surely he had thought
That now the Holy Grail would come again;
But sin broke out.   Ah, Christ, that it would come,
And heal the world of all their wickedness!
'O Father!' asked the maiden, 'might it come
To me by prayer and fasting?'   'Nay,' said he,
'I know not, for thy heart is pure as snow.'
And so she pray'd and fasted, till the sun
Shone, and the wind blew, thro' her, and I thought
She might have risen and floated when I saw her.

"For on a day she sent to speak with me.
And when she came to speak, behold her eyes
Beyond my knowing of them, beautiful,
Beyond all knowing of them, wonderful,
Beautiful in the light of holiness,
And 'O my brother, Percivale,' she said,

'Sweet brother, I have seen the Holy Grail:
For, waked at dead of night, I heard a sound
As of a silver horn from o'er the hills
Blown, and I thought, "It is not Arthur's use
To hunt by moonlight;" and the slender sound
As from a distance beyond distance grew
Coming upon me — O never harp nor horn,
Nor aught we blow with breath, or touch with hand,
Was like that music as it came; and then
Stream'd thro' my cell a cold and silver beam,
And down the long beam stole the Holy Grail,
Rose-red with beatings in it, as if alive,
Till all the white walls of my cell were dyed
With rosy colors leaping on the wall;
And then the music faded, and the Grail
Pass'd, and the beam decay'd, and from the walls
The rosy quiverings died into the night.
So now the Holy Thing is here again
Among us, brother, fast thou too and pray,
And tell thy brother knights to fast and pray,
That so perchance the vision may be seen
By thee and those, and all the world be heal'd.'

   "Then leaving the pale nun, I spake of this
To all men; and myself fasted and pray'd
Always, and many among us many a week
Fasted and pray'd even to the uttermost,
Expectant of the wonder that would be.

   "And one there was among us, ever moved
Among us in white armor, Galahad.

'God make thee good as thou art beautiful,'
Said Arthur, when he dubb'd him knight; and
      none,
In so young youth, was ever made a knight
Till Galahad; and this Galahad, when he heard
My sister's vision, fill'd me with amaze;
His eyes became so like her own, they seem'd
Hers, and himself her brother more than I.

"Sister or brother none had he; but some
Call'd him a son of Lancelot, and some said
Begotten by enchantment — chatterers they,
Like birds of passage piping up and down,
That gape for flies — we know not whence they
      come;
For when was Lancelot wanderingly lewd?

"But she, the wan sweet maiden, shore away
Clean from her forehead all that wealth of hair
Which made a silken mat-work for her feet;
And out of this she plaited broad and long
A strong sword-belt, and wove with silver thread
And crimson in the belt a strange device,
A crimson grail within a silver beam;
And saw the bright boy-knight, and bound it on
      him,
Saying, 'My knight, my love, my knight of heaven,
O thou, my love, whose love is one with mine,
I, maiden, round thee, maiden, bind my belt.
Go forth, for thou shalt see what I have seen,
And break thro' all, till one will crown thee king

Far in the spiritual city:' and as she spake
She sent the deathless passion in her eyes
Thro' him, and made him hers, and laid her mind
On him, and he believed in her belief.

"Then came a year of miracle: O brother,
In our great hall there stood a vacant chair,
Fashion'd by Merlin ere he past away,
And carven with strange figures; and in and out
The figures, like a serpent, ran the scroll
Of letters in a tongue no man could read.
And Merlin call'd it 'The Siege perilous,'
Perilous for good and ill; 'for there,' he said,
'No man could sit but he should lose himself:'
And once by misadvertence Merlin sat
In his own chair, and so was lost; but he,
Galahad, when he heard of Merlin's doom,
Cried, 'If I lose myself I save myself!'

"Then on a summer night it came to pass,
While the great banquet lay along the hall,
That Galahad would sit down in Merlin's chair.

"And all at once, as there we sat, we heard
A cracking and a riving of the roofs,
And rending, and a blast, and overhead
Thunder, and in the thunder was a cry.
And in the blast there smote along the hall
A beam of light seven times more clear than day:
And down the long beam stole the Holy Grail
All over cover'd with a luminous cloud,

And none might see who bare it, and it past.
But every knight beheld his fellow's face
As in a glory, and all the knights arose,
And staring each at other like dumb men
Stood, till I found a voice and sware a vow.

"I sware a vow before them all, that I,
Because I had not seen the Grail, would ride
A twelvemonth and a day in quest of it,
Until I found and saw it, as the nun
My sister saw it; and Galahad sware the vow,
And good Sir Bors, our Lancelot's cousin, sware,
And Lancelot sware, and many among the knights,
And Gawain sware, and louder than the rest."

Then spake the monk Ambrosius, asking him,
"What said the king?   Did Arthur take the vow?"

"Nay, my lord," said Percivale, "the King
Was not in hall: for early that same day,
'Scaped thro' a cavern from a bandit hold,
An outraged maiden sprang into the hall
Crying on help: for all her shining hair
Was smear'd with earth, and either milky arm
Red-rent with hooks of bramble, and all she wore
Torn as a sail that leaves the rope is torn
In tempest: so the King arose and went
To smoke the scandalous hive of those wild bees
That made such honey in his realm.   Howbeit
Some little of this marvel he too saw,
Returning o'er the plain that then began
To darken under Camelot: whence the King

Look'd up, calling aloud, 'Lo there! the roofs
Of our great Hall are rolled in thunder-smoke!
Pray Heaven, they be not smitten by the bolt.'
For dear to Arthur was that hall of ours,
As having there so oft with all his knights
Feasted, and as the stateliest under heaven.

   "O brother, had you known our mighty hall,
Which Merlin built for Arthur long ago!
For all the sacred mount of Camelot,
And all the dim rich city, roof by roof,
Tower after tower, spire beyond spire,
By grove, and garden-lawn, and rushing brook,
Climbs to the mighty hall that Merlin built.
And four great zones of sculpture, set betwixt
With many a mystic symbol, gird the hall:
And in the lowest beasts are slaying men,
And in the second men are slaying beasts,
And on the third are warriors, perfect men,
And on the fourth are men with growing wings,
And over all one statue in the mould
Of Arthur, made by Merlin, with a crown,
And peak'd wings pointed to the Northern Star.
And eastward fronts the statue, and the crown
And both the wings are made of gold, and flame
At sunrise till the people in far fields,
Wasted so often by the heathen hordes,
Behold it, crying, 'We have still a king.'

   "And, brother, had you known our hall within.
Broader and higher than any in all the lands!

Where twelve great windows blazon Arthur's wars,
And all the light that falls upon the board
Steams thro' the twelve great battles of our King.
Nay, one there is, and at the eastern end,
Wealthy with wandering lines of mount and mere,
Where Arthur finds the brand, Excalibur,
And also one to the west, and counter to it,
And blank : and who shall blazon it? when and
    how? —
O there, perchance, when all our wars are done,
The brand Excalibur will be cast away.

"So to this hall full quickly rode the King,
In horror lest the work by Merlin wrought,
Dreamlike, should on the sudden vanish, wrapt
In unremorseful folds of rolling fire.
And in he rode, and up I glanced, and saw
The golden dragon sparkling over all :
And many of those who burnt the hold, their arms
Hack'd, and their foreheads grimed with smoke,
    and sear'd,
Follow'd, and in among bright faces, ours,
Full of the vision, prest : and then the King
Spake to me, being nearest, 'Percivale,
(Because the hall was all in tumult — some
Vowing, and some protesting), 'what is this?'

"O brother, when I told him what had chanced,
My sister's vision, and the rest, his face
Darken'd, as I have seen it more than once,
When some brave deed seem'd to be done in vain,

Darken ; and 'Woe is me, my knights!' he cried,
'Had I been here, ye had not sworn the vow.'
Bold was mine answer, 'Had thyself been here,
My King, thou wouldst have sworn.' 'Yea, yea,'
    said he,
'Art thou so bold and hast not seen the Grail?'

  "'Nay, Lord, I heard the sound, I saw the light,
But since I did not see the Holy Thing,
I sware a vow to follow it till I saw.'

  "Then when he asked us, knight by knight, if
    any
Had seen it, all their answers were as one :
'Nay, Lord, and therefore have we sworn our vows.'

  "'Lo now,' said Arthur, 'have ye seen a cloud?
What go ye into the wilderness to see?'

  "Then Galahad on the sudden, and in a voice
Shrilling along the hall to Arthur, call'd,
'But I, Sir Arthur, saw the Holy Grail,
I saw the Holy Grail and heard a cry —
O Galahad, and O Galahad, follow me.'

  "'Ah, Galahad, Galahad,' said the King, 'for
    such
As thou art is the vision, not for these.
Thy holy nun and thou have seen a sign —
Holier is none, my Percivale, than she —
A sign to maim this Order which I made.
But you, that follow but the leader's bell,'

(Brother, the king was hard upon his knights,)
'Taliessin is our fullest throat of song,
And one hath sung and all the dumb will sing.
Lancelot is Lancelot, and hath overborne
Five knights at once, and every younger knight,
Unproven, holds himself as Lancelot,
Till overborne by one, he learns — and ye,
What are ye?   Galahads? — no, nor Percivales'
(For thus it pleased the King to range me close
After Sir Galahad); 'nay,' said he, 'but men
With strength and will to right .the wrong'd, of
    power
To lay the sudden head of violence flat,
Knights that in twelve great battles splash'd and
    dyed
The strong White Horse in his own heathen blood —
But one hath seen, and all the blind will see.
Go, since your vows are sacred being made:
Yet — for ye know the cries of all my realm,
Pass thro' this hall, — how often, O my knights,
Your places being vacant at my side,
This chance of noble deeds will come and go
Unchallenged, while you follow wandering fires
Lost in the quagmire? many of you, yea most,
Return no more: ye think I show myself
Too dark a prophet: come now, let us meet
The morrow morn once more in one full field
Of gracious pastime, that once more the king,
Before you leave him for this Quest, may count
The yet-unbroken strength of all his knights,
Rejoicing in that Order which he made.'

" So when the sun broke next from underground,
All the great table of our Arthur closed
And clash'd in such a tourney and so full,
So many lances broken — never yet
Had Camelot seen the like, since Arthur came;
And I myself and Galahad, for a strength
Was in us from the vision, overthrew
So many knights that all the people cried,
And almost burst the barriers in their heat,
Shouting, ' Sir Galahad and Sir Percivale!'

" But when the next day brake from under-
        ground —
O brother, had you known our Camelot,
Built by old kings, age after age, so old
The king himself had fears that it would fall,
So strange, and rich, and dim : for where the roofs
Totter'd toward each other in the sky,
Met foreheads all along the street of those
Who watch'd us pass ; and lower, and where the
        long
Rich galleries, lady-laden, weigh'd the necks
Of dragons clinging to the crazy walls,
Thicker than drops from thunder, showers of flowers
Fell as we past ; and men and boys astride
On wyvern, lion, dragon, griffin, swan,
At all the corners, named us each by name,
Calling ' God speed!' but in the street below
The knights and ladies wept, and rich and poor
Wept, and the King himself could hardly speak
For grief, and in the middle street the Queen,

Who rode by Lancelot, wail'd and shriek'd aloud,
' This madness has come on us for our sins.'
And then we reach'd the weirdly sculptured gate,
Where Arthur's wars were render'd mystically,
And thence departed every one his way.

" And I was lifted up in heart, and thought
Of all my late-shown prowess in the lists,
How my strong lance had beaten down the knights,
So many and famous names ; and never yet
Had heaven appear'd so blue, nor earth so green,
For all my blood danced in me, and I knew
That I should light upon the Holy Grail.

"Thereafter, the dark warning of our King,
That most of us would follow wandering fires,
Came like a driving gloom across my mind.
Then every evil word I had spoken once,
And every evil thought I had thought of old,
And every evil deed I ever did,
Awoke and cried, ' This Quest is not for thee.'
And lifting up mine eyes, I found myself
Alone, and in a land of sand and thorns,
And I was thirsty even unto death ;
And I, too, cried, ' This Quest is not for thee.'

" And on I rode, and when I thought my thirst
Would slay me, saw deep lawns, and then a brook,
With one sharp rapid, where the crisping white
Play'd ever back upon the sloping wave,
And took both ear and eye ; and o'er the brook

Were apple-trees, and apples by the brook
Fallen, and on the lawns, 'I will rest here,'
I said, 'I am not worthy of the Quest;'
But even while I drank the brook, and ate
The goodly apples, all these things at once
Fell into dust, and I was left alone,
And thirsting, in a land of sand and thorns.

   "And then behold a woman at a door
Spinning; and fair the house whereby she sat,
And kind the woman's eyes and innocent,
And all her bearing gracious; and she rose
Opening her arms to meet me, as who should say,
'Rest here;' but when I touch'd her, lo! she, too,
Fell into dust and nothing, and the house
Became no better than a broken shed,
And in it a dead babe; and also this
Fell into dust, and I was left alone.

   "And on I rode, and greater was my thirst.
Then flash'd a yellow gleam across the world,
And where it smote the ploughshare in the field,
The ploughman left his ploughing, and fell down
Before it; where it glitter'd on her pail,
The milkmaid left her milking, and fell down
Before it, and I knew not why, but thought
'The sun is rising,' tho' the sun had risen.
Then was I ware of one that on me moved
In golden armor with a crown of gold
About a casque all jewels; and his horse
In golden armor jewell'd everywhere:

And on the splendor came, flashing me blind;
And seem'd to me the Lord of all the world,
Being so huge.   But when I thought he meant
To crush me, moving on me, lo! he, too,
Opened his arms to embrace me as he came,
And up I went and touch'd him, and he, too,
Fell into dust, and I was left alone
And wearying in a land of sand and thorns.

"And I rode on and found a mighty hill,
And on the top, a city wall'd: the spires
Prick'd with incredible pinnacles into heaven.
And by the gateway stirr'd a crowd; and these
Cried to me climbing, 'Welcome, Percivale!
Thou mightiest and thou purest among men!'
And glad was I and clomb, but found at top
No man, nor any voice.   And thence I past
Far thro' a ruinous city, and I saw
That man had once dwelt there; but there I found
Only one man of an exceeding age.
'Where is that goodly company,' said I,
'That so cried out upon me?' and he had
Scarce any voice to answer, and yet gasp'd
'Whence and what art thou?' and even as he spoke
Fell into dust, and disappear'd, and I
Was left alone once more, and cried in grief,
'Lo, if I find the Holy Grail itself
And touch it, it will crumble into dust.'

"And thence I dropt into a lowly vale,
Low as the hill was high, and where the vale

Was lowest, found a chapel and thereby
A holy hermit in a hermitage,
To whom I told my phantoms, and he said:

  "'O son, thou hast not true humility,
The highest virtue, mother of them all;
For when the Lord of all things made Himself
Naked of glory for His mortal change,
"Take thou my robe," she said, "For all is thine."
And all her form shone forth with sudden light
So that the angels were amazed, and she
Follow'd him down, and like a flying star
Led on the gray-hair'd wisdom of the east;
But her thou hast not known: for what is this
Thou thoughtest of thy prowess and thy sins?
Thou hast not lost thyself to save thyself
As Galahad.' When the hermit made an end,
In silver armor suddenly Galahad shone
Before us, and against the chapel door
Laid lance, and enter'd, and we knelt in prayer.
And there the hermit slaked my burning thirst,
And at the sacring of the mass I saw
The holy elements alone; but he:
'Saw ye no more? I, Galahad, saw the Grail,
The Holy Grail, descend upon the shrine:
I saw the fiery face as of a child
That smote itself into the bread, and went;
And hither am I come; and never yet
Hath what my sister taught me first to see,
This Holy Thing, fail'd from my side nor come
Cover'd, but moving with me night and day,

Fainter by day, but always in the night
Blood-red, and sliding down the blacken'd marsh
Blood-red, and on the naked mountain top
Blood-red, and in the sleeping mere below
Blood-red.   And in the strength of this I rode,
Shattering all evil customs everywhere,
And past thro' Pagan realms, and made them mine,
And clashed with Pagan hordes, and bore them
      down,
And broke thro' all, and in the strength of this
Come victor.   But my time is hard at hand,
And hence I go; and one will crown me king
Far in the spiritual city; and come thou, too,
For thou shalt see the vision when I go.'

   " While thus he spake, his eye, dwelling on mine,
Drew me, with power upon me, till I grew
One with him, to believe as he believed.
Then, when the day began to wane, we went.

   " There rose a hill that none but man could climb,
Scarr'd with a hundred wintry watercourses —
Storm at the top, and when we gain'd it, storm
Round us and death; for every moment glanced
His silver arms and gloom'd: so quick and thick
The lightnings here and there to left and right
Struck, till the dry old trunks about us, dead,
Yea, rotten with a hundred years of death,
Sprang into fire: and at the base we found
On either hand, as far as eye could see,
A great black swamp and of an evil smell,

Part black, part whiten'd with the bones of men,
Not to be crost, save that some ancient king
Had built a way, where, link'd with many a bridge,
A thousand piers ran into the great Sea.
And Galahad fled along them bridge by bridge,
And every bridge as quickly as he crost
Sprang into fire and vanish'd, tho' I yearn'd
To follow; and thrice above him all the heavens
Open'd and blaz'd with thunder such as seem'd
Shoutings of all the sons of God: and first
At once I saw him far on the great Sea,
In silver-shining armor starry-clear;
And o'er his head the holy vessel hung
Clothed in white samite or a luminous cloud.
And with exceeding swiftness ran the boat,
If boat it were — I saw not whence it came.
And when the heavens open'd and blazed again
Roaring, I saw him like a silver star —
And had he set the sail, or had the boat
Become a living creature clad with wings?
And o'er his head the holy vessel hung
Redder than any rose, a joy to me,
For now I knew the veil had been withdrawn.
Then in a moment when they blazed again
Opening, I saw the least of little stars
Down on the waste, and straight beyond the star
I saw the spiritual city and all her spires
And gateways in a glory like one pearl —
No larger, tho' the goal of all the saints —
Strike from the sea; and from the star there shot
A rose-red sparkle to the city, and there

Dwelt, and I knew it was the Holy Grail,
Which never eyes on earth again shall see.
Then fell the floods of heaven drowning the deep.
And how my feet recross'd the deathful ridge
No memory in me lives; but that I touch'd
The chapel-doors at dawn I know; and thence
Taking my war-horse from the holy man,
Glad that no phantom vext me more, return'd
To whence I came, the gate of Arthur's wars."

"O brother," ask'd Ambrosius, — "for in sooth
These ancient books — and they would win thee —
    teem,
Only I find not there this Holy Grail,
With miracles and marvels like to these,
Not all unlike; which oftentime I read,
Who read but on my breviary with ease,
Till my head swims; and then go forth and pass
Down to the little thorpe that lies so close,
And almost plaster'd like a martin's nest
To these old walls — and mingle with our folk;
And knowing every honest face of theirs,
As well as ever shepherd knew his sheep,
And every homely secret in their hearts,
Delight myself with gossip and old wives,
And ills and aches, and teethings, lyings-in,
And mirthful sayings, children of the place,
That have no meaning half a league away:
Or lulling random squabbles when they rise,
Chafferings and chatterings at the market-cross,
Rejoice, small man, in this small world of mine.

Yea, even in their hens and in their eggs, —
O brother, saving this Sir Galahad
Came ye on none but phantoms in your quest,
No man, no woman?"

                    Then, Sir Percivale:
"All men, to one so bound by such a vow,
And women were as phantoms.   O my brother,
Why wilt thou shame me to confess to thee
How far I falter'd from my quest and vow?
For after I had lain so many nights
A bedmate of the snail and eft and snake,
In grass and burdock, I was changed to wan
And meagre, and the vision had not come,
And then I chanced upon a goodly town
With one great dwelling in the middle of it;
Thither I made, and there was I disarm'd
By maidens each as fair as any flower:
But when they led me into hall, behold
The Princess of that castle was the one,
Brother, and that one only, who had ever
Made my heart leap; for when I moved of old
A slender page about her father's hall,
And she a slender maiden, all my heart
Went after her with longing: yet we twain
Had never kiss'd a kiss, or vow'd a vow.
And now I came upon her once again,
And one had wedded her, and he was dead,
And all his land and wealth and state were hers.
And while I tarried, every day she set
A banquet richer than the day before

By me; for all her longing and her will
Was toward me as of old; till one fair morn,
I walking to and fro beside a stream
That flash'd across her orchard underneath
Her castle-walls, she stole upon my walk,
And calling me the greatest of all knights,
Embraced me, and so kiss'd me the first time,
And gave herself and all her wealth to me.
Then I remember'd Arthur's warning word,
That most of us would follow wandering fires,
And the Quest faded in my heart. Anon,
The heads of all her people drew to me,
With supplication both of knees and tongue.
'We have heard of thee: thou art our greatest
        knight:
Our Lady says it, and we well believe:
Wed thou our Lady, and rule over us,
And thou shalt be as Arthur in our land.'
O me, my brother! but one night my vow
Burnt me within, so that I rose and fled,
But wail'd and wept, and hated mine own self,
And ev'n the Holy Quest, and all but her;
Then after I was join'd with Galahad
Cared not for her, nor anything upon earth."

Then said the monk, "Poor men, when yule is
        cold,
Must be content to sit by little fires.
And this am I, so that ye care for me
Ever so little; yea, and blest be Heaven
That brought thee here to this poor house of ours,

Where all the brethren are so hard, to warm
My cold heart with a friend; and O the pity
To find thine own first love once more — to hold,
Hold her a wealthy bride within thine arms,
Or all but hold, and then — cast her aside,
Foregoing all her sweetness, like a weed.
For we that want the warmth of double life,
We that are plagued with dreams of something
        sweet
Beyond all sweetness in a life so rich, —
Ah, blessed Lord, I speak too earthly-wise,
Seeing I never stray'd beyond the cell,
But live like an old badger in his earth,
With earth about him everywhere, despite
All fast and penance.   Saw ye none beside,
None of your knights?"

                         "Yea so," said Percivale:
"One night my pathway swerving east, I saw
The pelican on the casque of our Sir Bors
All in the middle of the rising moon:
And toward him spurr'd and hail'd him, and he me,
And each made joy of either; than he ask'd,
'Where is he? hast thou seen him — Lancelot?
        Once,'
Said good Sir Bors, 'he dash'd across me — mad,
And maddening what he rode: and when I cried,
"Ridest thou then so hotly on a quest
So holy?" Lancelot shouted, "Stay me not!
I have been the sluggard, and I ride apace,
For now there is a lion in the way."
So vanish'd.'

" Then Sir Bors had ridden on
Softly, and sorrowing for our Lancelot,
Because his former madness, once the talk
And scandal of our table, had return'd ;
For Lancelot's kith and kin so worship him
That ill to him is ill to them ; to Bors
Beyond the rest : he well had been content
Not to have seen, so Lancelot might have seen,
The Holy Cup of healing ; and, indeed,
Being so clouded with his grief and love,
Small heart was his after the Holy Quest :
If God would send the vision, well : if not,
The Quest and he were in the hands of Heaven.

" And then, with small adventure met, Sir Bors
Rode to the lonest track of all the realm,
And found a people there among their crags,
Our race and blood, a remnant that were left
Paynim amid their circles, and the stones
They pitch up straight to heaven : and their wise
          men
Were strong in that old magic which can trace
The wandering of the stars, and scoff'd at him,
And this high Quest as at a simple thing :
Told him he follow'd — almost Arthur's words —
A mocking fire : ' what other fire than he,
Whereby the blood beats, and the blossom blows,
And the sea rolls, and all the world is warm'd ? '
And when his answer chafed them, the rough
          crowd,
Hearing he had a difference with their priests,

Seized him, and bound and plunged him into a cell
Of great piled stones; and lying bounden there
In darkness thro' innumerable hours
He heard the hollow-ringing heavens sweep
Over him, till by miracle — what else?
Heavy as it was, a great stone slipt and fell,
Such as no wind could move: and thro' the gap
Glimmer'd the streaming scud: then came a night
Still as the day was loud; and thro' the gap
The seven clear stars of Arthur's Table Round —
For, brother, so one night, because they roll
Thro' such a round in heaven, we named the stars,
Rejoicing in ourselves and in our king —
And these, like bright eyes of familiar friends,
In on him shone, 'And then to me, to me,'
Said good Sir Bors, 'beyond all hopes of mine,
Who scarce had pray'd or ask'd it for myself —
Across the seven clear stars — O grace to me —
In color like the fingers of a hand
Before a burning taper, the sweet Grail
Glided and past, and close upon it peal'd
A sharp quick thunder.' Afterwards a maid,
Who kept our holy faith among her kin
In secret, entering loosed and let him go."

To whom the monk: "And I remember now
That pelican on the casque: Sir Bors it was
Who spake so low and sadly at our board;
And mighty reverent at our grace was he:
A square-set man and honest: and his eyes,
An out-door sign of all the warmth within,

Smiled with his lips — a smile beneath a cloud,
But Heaven had meant it for a sunny one:
Ay, ay, Sir Bors, who else? But when ye reach'd
The city, found ye all your knights return'd,
Or was there sooth in Arthur's prophecy,
Tell me, and what said each, and what the King?

Then answer'd Percivale: "And that can I,
Brother, and truly: since the living words
Of so great men as Lancelot and our King
Pass not from door to door and out again,
But sit within the house. O, when we reach'd
The city, our horses stumbling as they trode
On heaps of ruin, hornless unicorns,
Crack'd basilisks, and splinter'd cockatrices,
And shatter'd talbots, which had left the stones
Raw, that they fell from, brought us to the hall.

"And there sat Arthur on the daïs-throne,
And those that had gone out upon the Quest,
Wasted and worn, and but a tithe of them,
And those that had not, stood before the King.
Who, when he saw me, rose, and bade me hail.
Saying, 'A welfare in thine eye reproves
Our fear of some disastrous chance for thee
On hill, or plain, at sea, or flooding ford.
So fierce a gale made havoc here of late
Among the strange devices of our kings;
Yea, shook this newer, stronger hall of ours,
And from the statue Merlin moulded for us
Half wrench'd a golden wing; but now — the quest,

This vision — hast thou seen the Holy Cup,
That Joseph brought of old to Glastonbury?'

  " So when I told him all thyself hast heard,
Ambrosius, and my fresh but fixt resolve
To pass away into the quiet life,
He answer'd not, but, sharply turning, ask'd
Of Gawain, 'Gawain, was this Quest for thee?'

  " ' Nay, lord,' said Gawain, 'not for such as I.
Therefore I communed with a saintly man,
Who made me sure the Quest was not for me.
For I was much awearied of the Quest ;
But found a silk pavilion in a field,
And merry maidens in it ; and then this gale
Tore my pavilion from the tenting-pin,
And blew my merry maidens all about
With all discomfort ; yea, and but for this,
My twelvemonth and a day were pleasant to me.'

  " He ceased ; and Arthur turn'd to whom at first
He saw not, for Sir Bors, on entering, push'd
Athwart the throng to Lancelot, caught his hand,
Held it, and there, half hidden by him, stood,
Until the King espied him, saying to him,
' Hail, Bors ! if ever loyal man and true
Could see it, thou hast seen the Grail ; ' and Bors,
' Ask me not, for I may not speak of it,
I saw it : ' and the tears were in his eyes —

  " Then there remain'd but Lancelot, for the rest
Spake but of sundry perils in the storm ;

Perhaps, like him of Cana in Holy Writ,
Our Arthur kept his best until the last.
'Thou, too, my Lancelot,' ask'd the King, 'my
    friend,
Our mightiest, hath this Quest avail'd for thee?'

  "'Our mightiest!' answer'd Lancelot, with a
    groan;
'O King!'—and when he paused, methought I
    spied
A dying fire of madness in his eyes,—
'O King, my friend, if friend of thine I be,
Happier are those that welter in their sin,
Swine in the mud, that cannot see for slime,
Slime of the ditch: but in me lived a sin
So strange, of such a kind, that all of pure,
Noble, and knightly in me twined and clung
Round that one sin, until the wholesome flower
And poisonous grew together, each as each,
Not to be pluck'd asunder; and when thy knights
Sware, I sware with them only in the hope
That could I touch or see the Holy Grail
They might be pluck'd asunder: then I spake
To one most holy saint, who wept and said,
That save they could be pluck'd asunder, all
My quest were but in vain; to whom I vow'd
That I would work according as he will'd.
And forth I went, and while I yearn'd and strove
To tear the twain asunder in my heart,
My madness came upon me as of old,
And whipt me into waste fields far away;

There was I beaten down by little men,
Mean knights, to whom the moving of my sword
And shadow of my spear had been enow
To scare them from me once; and then I came
All in my folly to the naked shore,
Wide flats, where nothing but coarse grasses grew;
But such a blast, my King, began to blow,
So loud a blast along the shore and sea,
Ye could not hear the waters for the blast,
Tho' heapt in mounds and ridges all the sea
Drove like a cataract, and all the sand
Swept like a river, and the clouded heavens
Were shaken with the motion and the sound.
And blackening in the sea-foam sway'd a boat,
Half swallow'd in it, anchor'd with a chain;
And in my madness to myself I said,
"I will embark and I will lose myself,
And in the great sea wash away my sin."
I burst the chain, I sprang into the boat.
Seven days I drove along the weary deep,
And with me drove the moon and all the stars;
And the wind fell, and on the seventh night
I heard the shingle grinding in the surge,
And felt the boat shock earth, and looking up,
Behold, the enchanted towers of Carbonek,
A castle like a rock upon a rock,
With chasm-like portals open to the sea,
And steps that met the breaker! there was none
Stood near it but a lion on each side
That kept the entry, and the moon was full.
Then from the boat I leapt, and up the stairs.

There drew my sword.   With sudden-flaring manes
Those two great beasts rose upright like a man,
Each gript a shoulder, and I stood between;
And when I would have smitten them, heard a voice,
"Doubt not, go forward; if thou doubt, the beasts
Will tear thee piecemeal;" then with violence
The sword was dash'd from out my hand, and fell.
And up into the sounding hall I past;
But nothing in the sounding hall I saw,
No bench nor table, painting on the wall
Or shield of knight; only the rounded moon
Thro' the tall oriel on the rolling sea.
But always in the quiet house I heard,
Clear as a lark, high o'er me as a lark,
A sweet voice singing in the topmost tower
To the eastward: up I climb'd a thousand steps
With pain: as in a dream I seem'd to climb
Forever: at the last I reach'd a door,
A light was in the crannies, and I heard,
"Glory and joy and honor to our Lord,
And to the Holy Vessel of the Grail."
Then in my madness I essay'd the door;
It gave, and thro' a stormy glare, a heat
As from a seventimes-heated furnace, I,
Blasted and burnt, and blinded as I was,
With such a fierceness that I swoon'd away —
O, yet methought I saw the Holy Grail,
All pall'd in crimson samite, and around
Great angels, awful shapes, and wings and eyes
And but for all my madness and my sin,
And then my swooning, I had sworn I saw

That which I saw; but what I saw was veil'd
And cover'd; and this quest was not for me.'

"So speaking, and here ceasing, Lancelot left
The hall long silent, till Sir Gawain — nay,
Brother, I need not tell thee foolish words, —
A reckless and irreverent knight was he,
Now bolden'd by the silence of his King.
Well, I will tell thee: 'O king, my liege,' he said,
'Hath Gawain fail'd in any quest of thine?
When have I stinted stroke in foughten field?
But as for thine, my good friend, Percivale,
Thy holy nun and thou have driven men mad,
Yea, made our mightiest madder than our least.
But by mine eyes and by mine ears I swear,
I will be deafer than the blue-eyed cat,
And thrice as blind as any noonday owl,
To holy virgins in their ecstasies,
Henceforward.'

"'Deafer,' said the blameless King,
'Gawain, and blinder unto holy things
Hope not to make thyself by idle vows,
Being too blind to have desire to see.
But if indeed there came a sign from heaven,
Blessed are Bors, Lancelot, and Percivale,
For these have seen according to their sight.
For every fiery prophet in old times,
And all the sacred madness of the bard,
When God made music thro' them, could but speak
His music by the framework and the chord;
And as ye saw it ye have spoken truth.

"'Nay — but thou errest, Lancelot: never yet
Could all of true and noble in knight and man
Twine round one sin, whatever it might be,
With such a closeness, but apart there grew,
Save that he were the swine thou spakest of,
Some root of knighthood and pure nobleness;
Whereto see thou, that it may bear its flower.

"'And spake I not too truly, O my knights?
Was I too dark a prophet when I said
To those who went upon the Holy Quest,
That most of them would follow wandering fires,
Lost in the quagmire? — lost to me and gone,
And left me gazing at a barren board,
And a lean Order — scarce return'd a tithe —
And out of those to whom the vision came
My greatest hardly will believe he saw;
Another hath beheld it afar off,
And leaving human wrongs to right themselves,
Cares but to pass into the silent life.
And one hath had the vision face to face,
And now his chair desires him here in vain,
However they may crown him otherwhere.

"'And some among you held, that if the King
Had seen the sight he would have sworn the vow:
Not easily, seeing that the King must guard
That which he rules, and is but as the hind,
To whom a space of land is given to plough,
Who may not wander from the allotted field
Before his work be done; but, being done,

Let visions of the night or of the day
Come, as they will; and many a time they come,
Until this earth he walks on seems not earth,
This light that strikes his eyeball is not light,
This air that smites his forehead is not air
But vision — yea, his very hands and feet —
In moments when he feels he cannot die,
And knows himself no vision to himself,
Nor the high God a vision, nor that One
Who rose again: ye have seen what ye have seen.

"So spake the King: I knew not all he meant."

CROSSING THE BAR.

SUNSET and evening star,
   And one clear call for me!
And may there be no moaning of the bar,
   When I put out to sea.

But such a tide as moving seems asleep,
   Too full for sound and foam,
When that which drew from out the boundless deep
   Turns again home.

Twilight and evening bell,
   And after that the dark!
And may there be no sadness of farewell,
   When I embark.

For tho' from out our bourne of Time and Place
   The flood may bear me far,
I hope to see my Pilot face to face
   When I have crossed the bar.